2016 SQA Past Papers With Answers

Higher
MODERN STUDIES

2014 Specimen Question Paper,
2015 & 2016 Exams

HODDER
GIBSON
AN HACHETTE UK COMPANY

This book contains the official 2014 SQA Specimen Question Paper, 2015 and 2016 Exams for Higher Modern Studies, with associated SQA-approved answers modified from the official marking instructions that accompany the paper.

In addition the book contains study skills advice. This advice has been specially commissioned by Hodder Gibson, and has been written by experienced senior teachers and examiners in line with the new Higher for CfE syllabus and assessment outlines. This is not SQA material but has been devised to provide further guidance for Higher examinations.

Hodder Gibson is grateful to the copyright holders, as credited on the final page of the Answer Section, for permission to use their material. Every effort has been made to trace the copyright holders and to obtain their permission for the use of copyright material. Hodder Gibson will be happy to receive information allowing us to rectify any error or omission in future editions.

Hachette UK's policy is to use papers that are natural, renewable and recyclable products and made from wood grown in sustainable forests. The logging and manufacturing processes are expected to conform to the environmental regulations of the country of origin.

Orders: please contact Bookpoint Ltd, 130 Park Drive, Milton Park, Abingdon, Oxon OX14 4SE. Telephone: (44) 01235 827720. Fax: (44) 01235 400454. Lines are open 9.00–5.00, Monday to Saturday, with a 24-hour message answering service. Visit our website at www.hoddereducation.co.uk. Hodder Gibson can be contacted direct on: Tel: 0141 333 4650; Fax: 0141 404 8188; email: hoddergibson@hodder.co.uk

This collection first published in 2016 by
Hodder Gibson, an imprint of Hodder Education,
An Hachette UK Company
211 St Vincent Street
Glasgow G2 5QY

Typeset by Aptara, Inc.

Printed in the UK

A catalogue record for this title is available from the British Library

ISBN: 978-1-4718-9099-4

3 2 1

2017 2016

Introduction

Study Skills – what you need to know to pass exams!

Pause for thought

Many students might skip quickly through a page like this. After all, we all know how to revise. Do you really though?

Think about this:

"IF YOU ALWAYS DO WHAT YOU ALWAYS DO, YOU WILL ALWAYS GET WHAT YOU HAVE ALWAYS GOT."

Do you like the grades you get? Do you want to do better? If you get full marks in your assessment, then that's great! Change nothing! This section is just to help you get that little bit better than you already are.

There are two main parts to the advice on offer here. The first part highlights fairly obvious things but which are also very important. The second part makes suggestions about revision that you might not have thought about but which WILL help you.

Part 1

DOH! It's so obvious but …

Start revising in good time

Don't leave it until the last minute – this will make you panic.

Make a revision timetable that sets out work time AND play time.

Sleep and eat!

Obvious really, and very helpful. Avoid arguments or stressful things too – even games that wind you up. You need to be fit, awake and focused!

Know your place!

Make sure you know exactly **WHEN and WHERE** your exams are.

Know your enemy!

Make sure you know what to expect in the exam.

How is the paper structured?

How much time is there for each question?

What types of question are involved?

Which topics seem to come up time and time again?

Which topics are your strongest and which are your weakest?

Are all topics compulsory or are there choices?

Learn by DOING!

There is no substitute for past papers and practice papers – they are simply essential! Tackling this collection of papers and answers is exactly the right thing to be doing as your exams approach.

Part 2

People learn in different ways. Some like low light, some bright. Some like early morning, some like evening / night. Some prefer warm, some prefer cold. But everyone uses their BRAIN and the brain works when it is active. Passive learning – sitting gazing at notes – is the most INEFFICIENT way to learn anything. Below you will find tips and ideas for making your revision more effective and maybe even more enjoyable. What follows gets your brain active, and active learning works!

Activity 1 – Stop and review

Step 1

When you have done no more than 5 minutes of revision reading STOP!

Step 2

Write a heading in your own words which sums up the topic you have been revising.

Step 3

Write a summary of what you have revised in no more than two sentences. Don't fool yourself by saying, "I know it, but I cannot put it into words". That just means you don't know it well enough. If you cannot write your summary, revise that section again, knowing that you must write a summary at the end of it. Many of you will have notebooks full of blue/black ink writing. Many of the pages will not be especially attractive or memorable so try to liven them up a bit with colour as you are reviewing and rewriting. **This is a great memory aid, and memory is the most important thing.**

Activity 2 – Use technology!

Why should everything be written down? Have you thought about "mental" maps, diagrams, cartoons and colour to help you learn? And rather than write down notes, why not record your revision material?

What about having a text message revision session with friends? Keep in touch with them to find out how and what they are revising and share ideas and questions.

Why not make a video diary where you tell the camera what you are doing, what you think you have learned and what you still have to do? No one has to see or hear it, but the process of having to organise your thoughts in a formal way to explain something is a very important learning practice.

Be sure to make use of electronic files. You could begin to summarise your class notes. Your typing might be slow, but it will get faster and the typed notes will be easier to read than the scribbles in your class notes. Try to add different fonts and colours to make your work stand out. You can easily Google relevant pictures, cartoons and diagrams which you can copy and paste to make your work more attractive and **MEMORABLE**.

Activity 3 – This is it. Do this and you will know lots!

Step 1

In this task you must be very honest with yourself! Find the SQA syllabus for your subject (www.sqa.org.uk). Look at how it is broken down into main topics called MANDATORY knowledge. That means stuff you MUST know.

Step 2

BEFORE you do ANY revision on this topic, write a list of everything that you already know about the subject. It might be quite a long list but you only need to write it once. It shows you all the information that is already in your long-term memory so you know what parts you do not need to revise!

Step 3

Pick a chapter or section from your book or revision notes. Choose a fairly large section or a whole chapter to get the most out of this activity.

With a buddy, use Skype, Facetime, Twitter or any other communication you have, to play the game "If this is the answer, what is the question?". For example, if you are revising Geography and the answer you provide is "meander", your buddy would have to make up a question like "What is the word that describes a feature of a river where it flows slowly and bends often from side to side?".

Make up 10 "answers" based on the content of the chapter or section you are using. Give this to your buddy to solve while you solve theirs.

Step 4

Construct a wordsearch of at least 10 × 10 squares. You can make it as big as you like but keep it realistic. Work together with a group of friends. Many apps allow you to make wordsearch puzzles online. The words and phrases can go in any direction and phrases can be split. Your puzzle must only contain facts linked to the topic you are revising. Your task is to find 10 bits of information to hide in your puzzle, but you must not repeat information that you used in Step 3. DO NOT show where the words are. Fill up empty squares with random letters. Remember to keep a note of where your answers are hidden but do not show your friends. When you have a complete puzzle, exchange it with a friend to solve each other's puzzle.

Step 5

Now make up 10 questions (not "answers" this time) based on the same chapter used in the previous two tasks. Again, you must find NEW information that you have not yet used. Now it's getting hard to find that new information! Again, give your questions to a friend to answer.

Step 6

As you have been doing the puzzles, your brain has been actively searching for new information. Now write a NEW LIST that contains only the new information you have discovered when doing the puzzles. Your new list is the one to look at repeatedly for short bursts over the next few days. Try to remember more and more of it without looking at it. After a few days, you should be able to add words from your second list to your first list as you increase the information in your long-term memory.

FINALLY! Be inspired...

Make a list of different revision ideas and beside each one write **THINGS I HAVE** tried, **THINGS I WILL** try and **THINGS I MIGHT** try. Don't be scared of trying something new.

And remember – "FAIL TO PREPARE AND PREPARE TO FAIL!"

Higher Modern Studies

The course

You will have studied the following three units:

- Democracy in Scotland and the United Kingdom
- Social Issues in the United Kingdom
- International Issues

Your teacher will usually have chosen one topic from each of the three sections above and you will answer questions on these in your exam (see table below).

Unit of the course	Option one	Option two
Democracy in Scotland and the UK	Democracy in Scotland	Democracy in the UK
Social Issues in the UK	Social Inequality	Crime and the Law
International Issues	World Powers	World Issues

Candidates are expected to complete three internal unit assessment items (part knowledge and understanding and part source-based). These must be completed to gain an overall course award.

The added value comes from the question paper and is an externally-marked assessment. This consists of two parts:

- Higher question paper

  60 marks allocated – two-thirds of marks
- Higher assignment

  30 marks allocated – one-third of marks

Total marks available = 90

The marks you achieve in the question paper and assignment are added together and an overall grade will be awarded. The grade is based on your total marks. Based on notional difficulty, 63 and above (70% and above) is an A; 54–62 (60%–69%) is a B; and 45–53 (50% to 59%) is a C.

The question paper

You will have 2 hours and 15 minutes to complete the question paper with a total of 60 marks allocated. There are three sections with each section worth 20 marks.

There are 16 marks available for skills-based questions and 44 marks for knowledge and understanding. These are assessed in three extended responses worth either 12 or 20 marks.

In the exam paper, more marks are awarded for knowledge and understanding than skills so it is crucial that you have a sound grasp of content.

Skills or source-based questions

There are two types of skills questions that you will have practised in class. Both are allocated 8 marks. These are:

1. Using up to three complex sources of information: **'to what extent is it accurate to state that…'**

2. Using up to three complex sources of information: **'what conclusions can be drawn…'**

As preparation for your exam, the best advice would be to practise source-based questions and to review the types of information required by an examiner for full marks. Remember, all the answers in source-based questions are contained within the sources. No marks are awarded for additional knowledge.

Knowledge (or extended response) questions

In the knowledge section of your exam you could be asked questions that have a similar style to the following:

- **Discuss – 20-mark extended response**, for example:

  The political system provides an effective check on the government.

  Discuss with reference to a world power you have studied.

- **To what extent – 20-mark extended response**, for example:

  To what extent has a world issue you have studied had an impact in different countries?

- **Evaluate – 12-mark extended response**, for example:

  > One aim of an electoral system is to provide fair representation.

  Evaluate the effectiveness of an electoral system you have studied in providing fair representation.

  You should refer to electoral systems used in Scotland or the United Kingdom or both in your answer.

- **Analyse – 12-mark extended response**, for example:

  Analyse the different lifestyle choices that may result in poor health.

Remember, in your course exam the knowledge questions for the International Issues section will not refer to a particular country or issue. You will be expected to base your answer around your knowledge and understanding of the World Power or World Issue you have studied.

Remember, also, in your course exam the two skills-based questions may appear in any two of the three sections. There will be no choice offered for skills-based questions. For example, if a skills-based question is examined in the Social Issues section, it will either be based on Social Inequality or Crime and the Law. The question is testing your skills and no knowledge is needed to answer the question.

What makes a good extended response answer?

- One that answers the question and only provides knowledge and understanding and analysis/ evaluation that is **relevant** to the question.
- One that is aware of the different requirements of a 20-mark and 12-mark answer. A 20-mark answer should include greater skills of analysis and evaluation and be more structured than a 12-mark answer.
- One that uses **up-to-date, relevant** examples to illustrate your understanding of the question being asked.
- One that includes a range of points with detailed exemplification and explanation, and analysis/ evaluation.
- For a 12-mark answer, one that includes knowledge/understanding and **either** analysis **or** evaluation. For a 20-mark response, one that includes knowledge/understanding, analysis, evaluation, a structure/line of argument and draws valid conclusions that address the question.

What makes a poor extended response answer?

- One that does not answer the question, or tries to change the question being asked. This is sometimes called "turning a question".
- One that gives detailed description or explanation that is not relevant to the question.
- One that contains information which is out of date.
- One that **only** provides a list of facts with no development or analysis/evaluation.

What makes a poor source-based answer?

- One that doesn't make use of all of the sources provided.
- One that fails to link information across sources.
- For the "objectivity" question, one that fails to make an overall judgement on the statement or fails to comment on the validity or reliability of the sources.
- For the "conclusions" question, one that fails to make an overall conclusion.

So you are now ready to answer the exam questions. Keep calm and don't panic.

Good luck!

National
Qualifications
SPECIMEN ONLY

SQ32/H/01

Modern Studies

Date — Not applicable

Duration — 2 hours and 15 minutes

Total marks — 60

SECTION 1 — DEMOCRACY IN SCOTLAND AND THE UNITED KINGDOM—20 marks

Attempt Question 1 and **EITHER** Question 2(a) **OR** 2(b)

SECTION 2 — SOCIAL ISSUES IN THE UNITED KINGDOM—20 marks
      Part A Social inequality in the United Kingdom
      Part B Crime and the law in the United Kingdom

Attempt Question 1 and **EITHER** Question 2(a) **OR** 2(b) **OR** 2(c) **OR** 2(d)

SECTION 3 — INTERNATIONAL ISSUES—20 marks
      Part A World powers
      Part B World issues

Attempt **EITHER** Question 1(a) **OR** 1(b) **OR** 1(c) **OR** 1(d)

Write your answers clearly in the answer booklet provided. In the answer booklet, you must clearly identify the question number you are attempting.

Use **blue** or **black** ink.

Before leaving the examination room you must give your answer booklet to the Invigilator; if you do not, you may lose all the marks for this paper.

SECTION 1 — DEMOCRACY IN SCOTLAND AND THE UNITED KINGDOM — 20 marks

Attempt Question 1 and **EITHER** Question 2(a) **OR** 2(b)

Question 1

Study Sources A and B below and opposite then attempt the question that follows.

SOURCE A

The 2010 General Election televised debates

The 2010 General Election witnessed the first live television debates between leaders from each of the three main UK parties — Conservatives, Labour and the Liberal Democrats. Cameron, Brown and Clegg all hoped to visually connect with voters during a tightly fought campaign nicknamed the 'digital election'.

Before the first-ever debate of its kind, an Ipsos MORI poll revealed 60% of those voters surveyed felt the TV debates would be important to them in helping decide the way they would vote. The performance of the candidates during the debates could also have the potential to alter the way the media would handle coverage of each of the leaders and their parties. Following the debates, a range of polls suggested Nick Clegg had won convincingly, with many voters indicating they would switch to the Liberal Democrats. The success of Nick Clegg led to claims of 'Cleggmania' and a prediction of a historic increase in the number of seats for the Liberal Democrats.

A second survey conducted after the election by an independent polling organisation found the leaders' TV debates changed the voting intentions of more than a million voters. Put another way, the results indicated that the debates altered the voting behaviour of more than 4% of the electorate. Also, it could be argued that TV coverage of the leaders' debate motivated thousands of voters to use their vote when otherwise they may not have done. In some parts of the country there was a rise of 17% in younger voters indicating that they would turn out to vote. On the other hand, it could be argued that the TV debates only reinforced the existing views most people had.

A third survey from the British Election Study 2010 found 9.4m people watched the first live debate on ITV, 4.5m watched the second debate on Sky and 8.5m the final debate on the BBC. After the second debate, polling figures suggested Cameron and Clegg were joint winners. After the third debate, polling figures suggested Cameron was the winner. Overall, the results from this study appeared to suggest 12% of voters changed their mind about which party to vote for as a consequence of watching the TV election debates.

After the polling stations closed and the votes were counted, it was found that no one party had an overall majority in the House of Commons. The Conservatives obtained the largest share of the overall vote polling 36% (up 3.7% from 2005), Labour attracted 29% of the vote (down 6.2% from 2005) and the Liberal Democrats 23% (up 1% from 2005).

(Adapted from various sources)

MARKS

Section 1 Question 1 (continued)

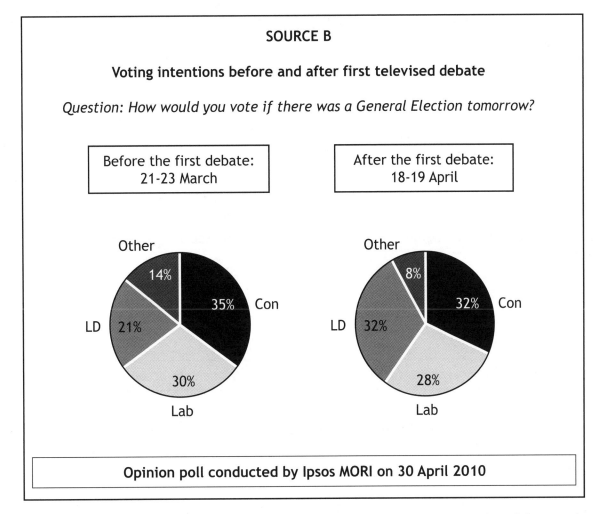

SOURCE B

Voting intentions before and after first televised debate

Question: How would you vote if there was a General Election tomorrow?

| Before the first debate: 21-23 March | After the first debate: 18-19 April |

Before the first debate:
- Other 14%
- Con 35%
- Lab 30%
- LD 21%

After the first debate:
- Other 8%
- Con 32%
- Lab 28%
- LD 32%

Opinion poll conducted by Ipsos MORI on 30 April 2010

Attempt the following question, using **only** the information in Sources A and B opposite and above.

To what extent is it accurate to state that the televised debates had a significant impact on voting intentions?

8

MARKS

Section 1 (continued)

Attempt **EITHER** Question 2(a) **OR** 2(b)

Question 2

(a)

> *One aim of an electoral system is to provide fair representation.*

Evaluate the effectiveness of an electoral system you have studied in providing fair representation.

You should refer to electoral systems used in Scotland **or** the United Kingdom **or** both in your answer.

12

OR

(b)

> *One role of parliamentary representatives is to hold the government to account.*

Evaluate the effectiveness of parliamentary representatives in holding the government to account.

You should refer to parliamentary representatives in Scotland **or** the United Kingdom **or** both in your answer.

12

SECTION 2 – SOCIAL ISSUES IN THE UNITED KINGDOM – 20 marks

MARKS

Attempt Question 1 and **EITHER** Question 2(a) **OR** 2(b) **OR** 2(c) **OR** 2(d)

Question 1

Study Sources A, B and C then attempt the question which follows.

SOURCE A

Social exclusion

Social exclusion is a term used to describe a person or group that lacks sufficient income to play a full part in society. For example, those socially excluded may not have enough money for special celebrations such as birthdays, for toys and books for children or for warm winter clothing. Those people experiencing social exclusion are most likely to be affected by low income, poor health, unemployment, fuel poverty and poor housing. The problems linked with social exclusion are something that both the Scottish and UK governments have been concerned to address in recent years.

Generally, although Scots are living longer, premature death and crime rates are falling and unemployment rates have also started to fall. However, social exclusion continues to impact on the lives of many Scottish citizens. The wealthiest groups in Scotland continue to lead better lives and the gap between the best and worst off in Scotland continues to widen.

Those who are worst off in Scottish society are less likely to access health services than those who are better off and usually have higher death and illness rates. Low life expectancy rates and long-term illness are often strong indicators of people experiencing social exclusion.

Evidence suggests that those people suffering social exclusion are not equally spread across Scotland. There are significant differences in health, earnings, crime and employment levels between Scottish local authorities and between urban and rural areas.

SOURCE B
Premature death rates for people under 65 years of age by selected Scottish local authority area per 100,000

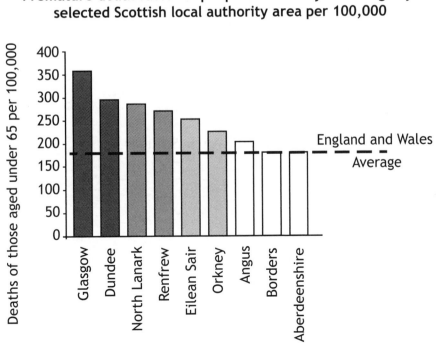

Section 2 Question 1 (continued)

SOURCE C

Social and economic data from selected Scottish local authorities

Rural areas	Urban areas
Aberdeenshire	**Dundee City**
• Average gross earnings per week: £570·60 • Unemployment rate: 1·5% • Crime rate per 10,000 people: 286 • Employment rate: 79·6% • Life expectancy: 78·2 years • Long-standing illness: 11% • National percentage share of the poorest parts of the country: 0%	• Average gross earnings per week: £483·30 • Unemployment rate: 5·9% • Crime rate per 10,000 people: 616 • Employment rate: 68·4% • Life expectancy: 73·9 years • Long-standing illness: 17% • National percentage share of the poorest parts of the country: 5·8%
Borders	**Glasgow City**
• Average gross earnings per week: £430·11 • Unemployment rate: 3·3% • Crime rate per 10,000 people: 281 • Employment rate: 73·1% • Life expectancy: 77·5 years • Long-standing illness: 12% • National percentage share of the poorest parts of the country: 0·3%	• Average gross earnings per week: £506 • Unemployment rate: 5·8% • Crime rate per 10,000 people: 889 • Employment rate: 63·8% • Life expectancy: 71·6 years • Long-standing illness: 22% • National percentage share of the poorest parts of the country: 45%

Attempt the following question, using **only** the information in Sources A, B and C opposite and above.

What conclusions can be drawn about social exclusion in Scotland?

You must draw conclusions about:

- the links between social exclusion and health
- the links between social exclusion and local authority area

You must give an overall conclusion on social exclusion in Scotland.

8

MARKS

Section 2 (continued)

Attempt **EITHER** Question 2(a) **OR** 2(b) **OR** 2(c) **OR** 2(d)

Question 2

Part A: Social inequality in the United Kingdom

Answers may refer to Scotland **or** the United Kingdom **or** both.

(a) Analyse government policies to tackle inequalities that affect a group in society.   **12**

OR

(b) Analyse the different lifestyle choices that may result in poor health.   **12**

OR

Part B: Crime and the law in the United Kingdom

Answers may refer to Scotland **or** the United Kingdom **or** both.

(c) Analyse government policies to tackle crime.   **12**

OR

(d) Analyse the ways in which the victims of crime are affected.   **12**

MARKS

SECTION 3 — INTERNATIONAL ISSUES — 20 marks

Attempt **EITHER** Question 1(a) **OR** 1(b) **OR** 1(c) **OR** 1(d)

Question 1

Part A: World powers

(a) *The political system provides an effective check on the government.*

Discuss with reference to a world power you have studied. **20**

OR

(b) To what extent does a world power you have studied have influence in international relations? **20**

OR

Part B: World issues

(c) *International organisations have been successful in resolving a significant world issue.*

Discuss with reference to a world issue you have studied. **20**

OR

(d) To what extent has a world issue you have studied had an impact in different countries? **20**

[END OF SPECIMEN QUESTION PAPER]

HIGHER

2015

National
Qualifications
2015

X749/76/11

Modern Studies

WEDNESDAY, 27 MAY

9:00 AM – 11:15 AM

Total marks — 60

SECTION 1 — DEMOCRACY IN SCOTLAND AND THE
UNITED KINGDOM — 20 marks

Attempt **EITHER** Question 1(a) **OR** 1(b)

SECTION 2 — SOCIAL ISSUES IN THE UNITED KINGDOM — 20 marks
  Part A Social inequality in the United Kingdom
  Part B Crime and the law in the United Kingdom

Attempt Question 2 and **EITHER** Question 3(a) **OR** 3(b) **OR** 3(c) **OR** 3(d)

SECTION 3 — INTERNATIONAL ISSUES — 20 marks
  Part A World Powers
  Part B World Issues

Attempt Question 4 and **EITHER** Question 5(a) **OR** 5(b) **OR** 5(c) **OR** 5(d)

Write your answers clearly in the answer booklet provided. In the answer booklet, you must clearly identify the question number you are attempting.

Use **blue** or **black** ink.

Before leaving the examination room you must give your answer booklet to the Invigilator; if you do not, you may lose all the marks for this paper.

MARKS

SECTION 1 — DEMOCRACY IN SCOTLAND AND THE UNITED KINGDOM — 20 marks

Attempt **EITHER** Question 1(a) **OR** 1(b)

Question 1

(a)

Some factors are more important than others in influencing voting behaviour.

To what extent are some factors more important than others in influencing voting behaviour?

You should refer to voting behaviour in Scotland **or** the United Kingdom **or** both in your answer.

20

OR

(b)

Most citizens participate effectively in the political process.

Discuss.

You should refer to participation in Scotland **or** the United Kingdom **or** both in your answer.

20

[Turn over for SECTION 2 on *Page four*]

DO NOT WRITE ON THIS PAGE

SECTION 2 — SOCIAL ISSUES IN THE UNITED KINGDOM — 20 marks

Attempt Question 2 and **EITHER** Question 3(a) **OR** 3(b) **OR** 3(c) **OR** 3(d)

Question 2

Study Sources A, B and C then attempt the question which follows.

SOURCE A

Reducing smoking remains a challenge

Despite the ban on smoking in enclosed public places which came into force in 2006, smoking still accounts for more than 13,000 deaths in Scotland each year and is the main cause of early death. Treating people with smoking related conditions costs NHS Scotland about £271 million each year. Smoking in young people can lead to addiction and damage to their hearts and lungs. Almost 600 children — some as young as 11 — take up smoking every day across the UK. Figures from Cancer Research UK estimate that 463 children start smoking every day in England, 50 in Scotland, 30 in Wales and 19 in Northern Ireland. These habits, if continued into adulthood, can lead to further ill health and can affect a person's ability to work.

Tobacco has financial costs as well as health costs for young smokers, with a pack of 20 cigarettes costing around £8. Survey data from Scotland shows that 17% of both 13 and 15 year old regular smokers i.e. those who smoke at least once per week, spend more than £20 per week on cigarettes. In Scotland, 39% of those in the most deprived areas smoke, compared to just 10% in the least deprived areas.

The government has introduced legislation aimed at reducing the number of people who take up smoking. This includes changes to the ways cigarettes can be displayed in supermarkets, removing cigarette vending machines from pubs and raising the age to buy cigarettes to 18 years.

The Scottish Government has also proposed other policies to reduce smoking, aiming for Scotland to be tobacco free by 2034. Before then, plans include the introduction of plain packaging, smoke free hospital grounds and additional funding for education programmes which try to stop young people from taking up smoking in the first place.

In 2013, less than one quarter of Scottish adults smoked. This continues a downward trend in this figure. Smoking rates differ depending where you live in the UK. Scotland reported the highest proportion of current smokers with 23%. This compared to 19% in England, 21% in Wales and 19% in Northern Ireland. However, those groups who are out of work and rely on benefits for their income remain the most likely groups to smoke.

Source: Adapted from bbc.co.uk (March 2013) and Cancer Research UK

SOURCE B — Percentage (%) who smoke in Scotland by economic status* (2012)   MARKS

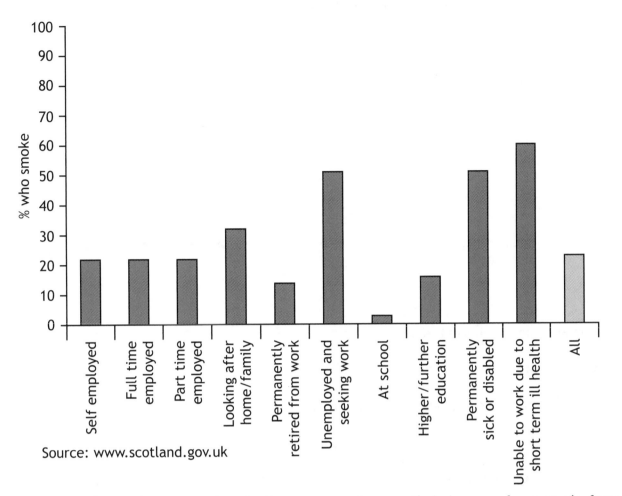

Source: www.scotland.gov.uk

Note: Economic status refers to the ways people earn their income, for example from earnings if working or through Social Security benefits if unemployed or disabled.

SOURCE C — Percentage (%) of 13 and 15 year olds who smoke regularly 1990-2013 and 2014-2018 (projected)

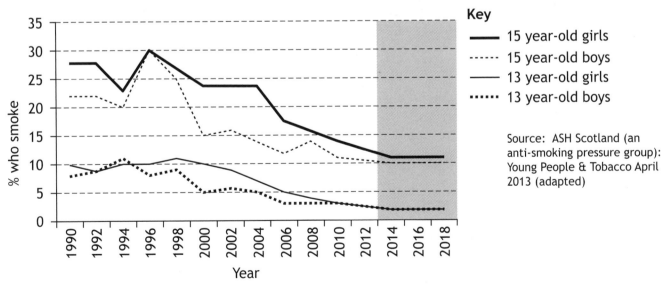

Key
— 15 year-old girls
···· 15 year-old boys
— 13 year-old girls
▪▪▪▪ 13 year-old boys

Source: ASH Scotland (an anti-smoking pressure group): Young People & Tobacco April 2013 (adapted)

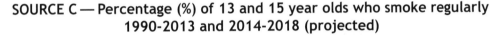

Attempt the following question, using **only** the information in Sources A, B and C opposite and above.

To what extent is it accurate to state that the government's policies are successfully tackling the problem of smoking in Scotland?   **8**

MARKS

Attempt **EITHER** Question 3(a) **OR** 3(b) **OR** 3(c) **OR** 3(d)

Question 3

Part A: Social inequality in the United Kingdom

Answers may refer to Scotland **or** the United Kingdom **or** both.

(a) Evaluate the view that social inequality affects some groups in society more than others.

12

OR

(b) Evaluate the effectiveness of **either** the benefits system **or** health services in tackling social inequality.

12

OR

Part B: Crime and the law in the United Kingdom

Answers may refer to Scotland **or** the United Kingdom **or** both.

(c) Evaluate the view that crime only affects the victims.

12

OR

(d) Evaluate the effectiveness of **either** prison sentences **or** community based sentences in tackling crime.

12

[Turn over for SECTION 3 on *Page eight*]

DO NOT WRITE ON THIS PAGE

SECTION 3 — INTERNATIONAL ISSUES — 20 marks

Attempt Question 4 and **EITHER** Question 5(a) **OR** 5(b) **OR** 5(c) **OR** 5(d)

Question 4

Study Sources A, B and C then attempt the question which follows.

SOURCE A

The Recession and The Eurozone

When the Euro launched in 1999 it became the official currency of 11 European Union (EU) member countries. Gradually, more countries saw the Euro's benefits and adopted it as their currency. Today over 336 million people in 19 countries use it and form what we call the Eurozone. Nine EU countries have not joined the Eurozone.

During the recession which began in 2008, the Euro struggled to compete against stronger currencies such as the dollar which led to some countries reporting a series of long term economic problems.

As a result of the recession, across the EU, many businesses lost sales and cut jobs. The unemployment rate throughout the EU went from 7% in 2008 to 10% in 2014 with an estimated 24·5 million people out of work.

Some Eurozone members have required financial hand-outs to help them cope with their growing level of debt. In May 2010 Greece received 110 billion Euros followed by 130 billion Euros in 2012. Ireland and Spain have also benefited from a 90 billion Euro hand-out. Portugal received financial assistance twice within the space of a year. However, some Eurozone countries such as Germany have benefited from using the Euro to build up trade and generate income, which has kept their debt levels comparatively low. In the EU, debt went from 63% of Gross Domestic Product* (GDP) in 2008 to 89% of GDP in 2014.

Largely because of an increase in part time jobs, the UK's economy has not suffered as badly as some other Non-Eurozone members in terms of unemployment. Some other Non-Eurozone countries have not seen big increases in unemployment as many of their young people have moved to other countries in order to find work.

The Eurozone is a huge market for businesses from the United States, China, India, Japan, Russia and other major world economic powers who have been affected by the recession despite not being EU members. In 2008 these five powers purchased 41% of EU exports. By 2014 this figure was 37%. The collapse of the Euro or a situation where countries are unable to repay their debt could trigger a further world-wide recession.

*Gross Domestic Product – total value of goods and services produced in one country

SOURCE B

Unemployment Rates (%) — Selected Eurozone members

Country	(2008)	(2014)
Ireland	6·4	11
Greece	7·7	25·9
Portugal	8·5	15·3
Spain	11·3	25·6
Cyprus	3·7	15·3

Government Debt — Selected Eurozone members
(National debt as a percentage of GDP)

Country	(2008)	(2014)
Ireland	25%	123%
Greece	105%	175%
Portugal	68%	129%
Spain	36%	72%
Cyprus	59%	112%

SOURCE C

Unemployment Rates (%) — Selected Non-Eurozone members

Country	(2008)	(2014)
UK	5·6	6
Sweden	6·2	8·1
Denmark	3·5	7
Poland	7·1	9·2
Romania	5·8	7·2

Government Debt — Selected Non-Eurozone members
(National debt as a percentage of GDP)

Country	(2008)	(2014)
UK	44%	90%
Sweden	40%	40%
Denmark	27%	44%
Poland	45%	57%
Romania	13%	38%

Attempt the following question, using **only** the information in Sources A, B and C opposite and above.

What conclusions can be drawn about the impact of the recession on different EU members?

You must draw conclusions about:

- the impact of the recession on Eurozone members
- the impact of the recession on Non-Eurozone members

You must now give an overall conclusion about the impact of the recession on the EU.

8

MARKS

Section 3 (continued)

Attempt **EITHER** Question 5(a) **OR** 5(b) **OR** 5(c) **OR** 5(d)

Question 5

Part A: World Powers

With reference to a world power you have studied:

(a) Analyse the ability of this world power to influence other countries.   **12**

OR

(b) Analyse the impact of a recent social issue on this world power.   **12**

OR

Part B: World Issues

With reference to a world issue you have studied:

(c) Analyse the role of international organisations in attempting to resolve this issue.   **12**

OR

(d) Analyse the different factors which have caused this issue.   **12**

[END OF QUESTION PAPER]

HIGHER

2016

MONDAY, 30 MAY

9:00 AM – 11:15 AM

Total marks — 60

SECTION 1 — DEMOCRACY IN SCOTLAND AND THE UNITED KINGDOM — 20 marks

Attempt Question 1 and **EITHER** Question 2(a) **OR** 2(b)

SECTION 2 — SOCIAL ISSUES IN THE UNITED KINGDOM — 20 marks

        Part A Social inequality in the United Kingdom
        Part B Crime and the law in the United Kingdom

Attempt **EITHER** Question 3(a) **OR** 3(b) **OR** 3(c) **OR** 3(d)

SECTION 3 — INTERNATIONAL ISSUES — 20 marks

        Part A World Powers
        Part B World Issues

Attempt Question 4 and **EITHER** Question 5(a) **OR** 5(b) **OR** 5(c) **OR** 5(d)

Write your answers clearly in the answer booklet provided. In the answer booklet you must clearly identify the question number you are attempting.

Use **blue** or **black** ink.

Before leaving the examination room you must give your answer booklet to the Invigilator; if you do not, you may lose all the marks for this paper.

SECTION 1 – DEMOCRACY IN SCOTLAND AND THE UNITED KINGDOM – 20 marks

Attempt Question 1 and **EITHER** Question 2(a) **OR** 2(b)

Question 1

Study Sources A, B and C then attempt the question which follows.

SOURCE A

Political Inequality in the UK and why Voting Matters

A central claim of democracy is that every citizen's preference, no matter what their socio-economic status, should count equally. There are, however, good reasons for supposing that the principle of political equality and democracy are under threat and that politics is increasingly becoming the preserve of the rich and the powerful. In Britain, there is a growing public belief that some groups in the British population are better represented politically than others. There is a widespread suspicion that governments are more likely to pass laws which benefit the groups most likely to vote.

A great problem facing British democracy is the growing inequality within voter turnout. Although overall turnout was 66·1% in 2015, electoral participation is lower among lower income groups, mainly Social Classes D and E. This gives better-off voters, mainly in Social Classes A and B, disproportionate influence at the ballot box.

Unequal turnout reinforces a vicious cycle of disaffection and under-representation among those groups where electoral participation is falling. As government policy becomes less responsive to their interests the less inclined they will be to vote. The less they vote, the less likely governments will respond to their interests; thus establishing a downward spiral excluding poorer socio-economic groups from electoral life.

Those who vote at their first eligible election are considerably more likely to vote throughout the duration of their life. Forcing young people to turnout at the ballot box is one option that might break the non-voting habit plaguing our youth and would have a substantial impact on voter turnout as each generation ages. However, Scotland managed to engage its younger generation during the 2014 Independence Referendum without compulsory voting. The subsequent 7% increase in Scottish turnout at the 2015 General Election was largely responsible for the small increase in turnout across the whole UK.

SOURCE B
UK General Election Statistics

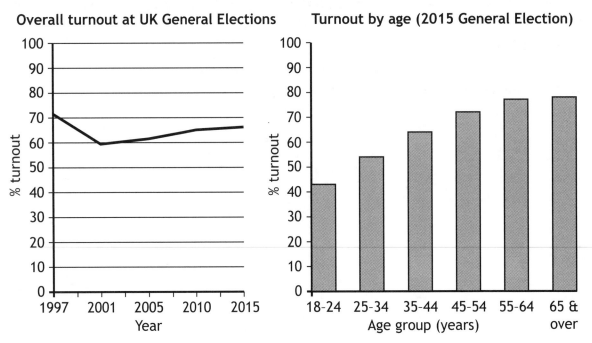

Source B (continued)

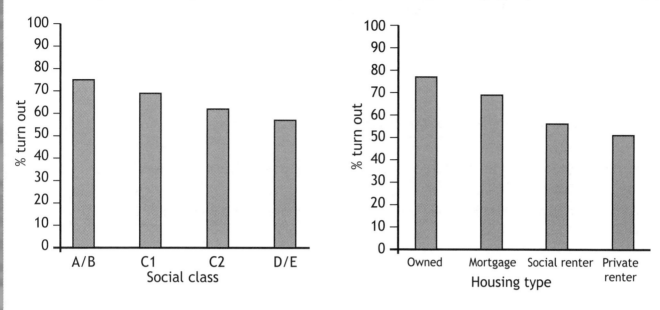

Turnout by Social Class (2015 General Election)   Turnout by Housing type (2015 General Election)

SOURCE C

Selected Government Policies (Introduced between the 2010 and 2015 General Elections)

Policy	Description
VAT increased to 20%	Disproportionately affected poorest households more than middle to upper income levels
End of Educational Maintenance Allowance (EMA) in England and Wales	Removal of Government financial aid to help pupils from poorer backgrounds to stay on at school
Child Tax Credit	Households earning more than £40,000 per year will not receive this
Cap on Benefits	Households in receipt of benefits will receive no more than average UK family income
Bedroom Tax	Removal of some benefit for those staying in rented housing that has excess bedroom capacity
Flat Rate State Pension/ Retirement Age	Increase from £97 per week to £140 for single pensioners and an increase in retirement age to 68
Child Benefit means tested	Those earning over £50,000 will no longer receive this benefit
Housing Benefit	Under 26s no longer allowed to claim this benefit
Top Rate Tax Cut	5% reduction in tax levels for those earning more than £150,000 per year

Attempt the following question, using **only** the information in Sources A, B and C on *Page 02 and above.*

What conclusions can be drawn about turnout in the UK?

You **must** draw **one** conclusion about each of the following;

- the link between government policy and the turnout of different age groups
- the link between government policy and the turnout of different socio-economic groups

You **must** give an overall conclusion about turnout in the UK.   **8**

Section 1 (continued)

Attempt **EITHER** Question 2(a) **OR** 2(b)

Question 2

(a)

Electoral systems allow the views of the electorate to be represented.

Analyse the ways in which an electoral system you have studied allows the views of the electorate to be represented.

You should refer to an electoral system used in Scotland **or** the United Kingdom **or** both in your answer.

12

OR

(b)

Individuals and groups in society can influence government decision making in many ways.

Analyse the ways in which individuals and groups in society can influence government decision making.

You should refer to individuals and groups in Scotland **or** the United Kingdom **or** both in your answer.

12

MARKS

SECTION 2 – SOCIAL ISSUES IN THE UNITED KINGDOM – 20 marks

Attempt **EITHER** question 3(a) **OR** 3(b) **OR** 3(c) **OR** 3(d)

Question 3

Part A: Social inequality in the United Kingdom

Answers may refer to Scotland **or** the United Kingdom **or** both.

(a) Government policies have failed to reduce social inequalities.
Discuss.   **20**

OR

(b) To what extent can ill-health be blamed on the lifestyle choices of the population?   **20**

OR

Part B: Crime and the law in the United Kingdom

Answers may refer to Scotland **or** the United Kingdom **or** both.

(c) Government policies have failed to reduce crime.
Discuss.   **20**

OR

(d) To what extent is human nature the main cause of crime?   **20**

[Turn over

SECTION 3 — INTERNATIONAL ISSUES — 20 marks

Attempt Question 4 and **EITHER** Question 5(a) **OR** 5(b) **OR** 5(c) **OR** 5(d)

Question 4

Study Sources A, B and C then attempt the question which follows.

SOURCE A

Russia's "Foreign Agents"

In 2012 Russia's parliament adopted a law that required campaign groups to register as "foreign agents" with the Ministry of Justice if they engaged in "political activity" and received foreign funding. The definition of "political activity" under the law is so broad and vague that it covered almost all campaign groups in Russia.

Russian authorities arrested and harassed activists, blocked independent online media and proposed measures that would further stifle free expression. More recently pro-government media published material blaming the government of Ukraine for the on-going civil war in that country, trying to deflect attention away from Russia's invasion and occupation of Crimea.

In Russia "foreign agent" is interpreted as "spy" or "traitor." The groups campaigning for political freedoms were in no doubt that the law aimed to demonise them, and to turn the public against them. Russia's many human rights groups boycotted the law, calling it "slanderous." Many of them have now been forced to disband and many of their leaders have been prosecuted for refusing to register as a "foreign agent". In the past such individuals may have faced the death sentence but Russia has not executed anyone since 1996.

In August 2013, four organisations challenged the law in Russia's Constitutional Court. On April 8, 2014 the court upheld the law, ruling that the term "foreign agent" had no negative connotations, therefore, its use was "not intended to persecute or discredit" anyone. The court also found that labelling campaign groups as "foreign agents" was in the interests of state security and did not affect the right to protest. The ruling has been heavily criticised by many foreign governments.

Source: Adapted from the website of an international pressure group campaigning to improve human rights.

SOURCE B

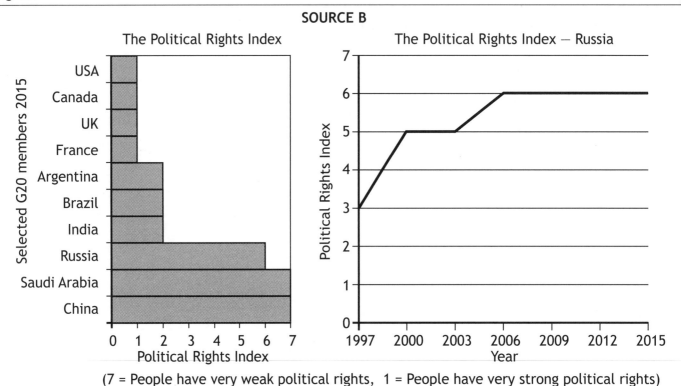

The Political Rights Index

The Political Rights Index — Russia

(7 = People have very weak political rights, 1 = People have very strong political rights)

Source: Adapted from an academic website for students and teachers of international affairs.

Note: The Political Rights Index measures how free and fair elections are, the right to free speech and to campaign, and the fairness of government departments including the police, courts and prisons.

MARKS

SOURCE C

Annual Report 2014

"There have been fewer complaints from Russians over human rights violations", Government spokesman Vladimir Lukin said in his annual report. He said that more than half of the complaints he had received last year were about violations of civil rights and freedoms. The number of complaints concerning political rights was relatively small, and complaints about religious freedoms and freedom of conscience decreased by 10%.

In 2014, Mr Lukin's offices received 24,000 complaints; in 2012 the figure was 58,000. Many people were worried about violations of their personal rights, others complained about unfair court rulings; more than half of the letters (56%) were complaints about the courts and nearly one-quarter of the complaints were about abuses by the police or prison staff. As for political complaints, they accounted for 2% of the total. Lukin also praised a recent report by the European Union which congratulated Russia on its expansion of jury trials right across Russia and its suspension of the death penalty.

As he submitted his report to President Vladimir Putin, Lukin brought up the issue of mass inspections of human rights groups, launched in recent weeks. Lukin assured the journalists that political campaign groups had nothing to fear and that their right to protest was protected by Russian law.

Source: Adapted from the website of the Russian Government's news agency.

Attempt the following question, using **only** the information in Sources A, B and C on *Page six* and above.

To what extent is it accurate to state that Russia effectively protects the rights of its citizens?

In your answer, you may wish to evaluate the reliability of the sources.

8

[Turn over for next question

MARKS

Section 3 (continued)

Attempt **EITHER** Question 5(a) **OR** 5(b) **OR** 5(c) **OR** 5(d)

Part A: World Powers

With reference to a world power you have studied:

(a) Evaluate the success of the Government in tackling a socio-economic issue.   **12**

OR

(b) Evaluate the effectiveness of the political system in representing the wishes of the population.   **12**

OR

Part B: World Issues

With reference to a world issue you have studied:

(c) Evaluate the impact of this issue on the individuals and groups affected.   **12**

OR

(d) Evaluate the effectiveness of international organisations in addressing this issue.   **12**

[END OF QUESTION PAPER]

Answers

SQA HIGHER
MODERN STUDIES 2016

General Marking Principles for Higher Modern Studies

Marking principles for each question type

For each of the question types the following provides an overview of marking principles.

The types of questions used in this paper are:
- Discuss ... [20 marks extended response]
- To what extent ... [20 marks extended response]
- Evaluate ... [12 marks extended response]
- Analyse ... [12 marks extended response]
- To what extent is it accurate to state that ... [information-handling question — 8 marks]
- What conclusions can be drawn ... [information-handling question — 8 marks]

Extended response (12 or 20 marks)

For 12 marks responses, up to a maximum of **8 marks** will be awarded for knowledge and understanding (description, explanation and exemplification). The remaining marks will be awarded for the demonstration of higher-order skills of analysis or evaluation. Where a candidate makes more analytical/evaluative points than are required to gain the maximum allocation of **4 marks**, these can be credited as knowledge and understanding marks provided they meet the criteria for this.

For 20 marks responses, up to **8 marks** will be awarded for knowledge and understanding (description, explanation and exemplification). The remaining marks will be awarded for the demonstration of higher-order skills of analysis and evaluation and structured argument. Where a candidate makes more analytical/evaluative points than are required to gain the maximum allocation of marks, these can be credited as knowledge and understanding marks provided they meet the criteria for this.

In the *Democracy in Scotland and the United Kingdom* and the *Social Issues in the United Kingdom* sections, candidates should be credited for responses which refer to Scotland only, to the United Kingdom only, or to both Scotland and the United Kingdom in their responses.

Analyse questions
- Candidates will identify parts of an issue, the relationship between these parts and their relationships with the whole; draw out and relate implications.

Evaluate questions
- Candidates will make a judgement based on criteria; determine the value of something.

Discuss questions
- Candidates will communicate ideas and information on the issue in the statement. Candidates will be credited for analysing and evaluating different views of the statement/ viewpoint.

To what extent questions
- Candidates will analyse the issue in the question and come to a conclusion or conclusions which involve an evaluative judgement which is likely to be quantitative in nature.

Source-based questions that assess information-handling skills (8 marks)
- Questions will have at least two sources at an appropriate SCQF level.
- Award up to **3 marks** for a single developed point depending on the use of the evidence in the sources and the quality of the analysis/evaluation.
- Credit candidates who synthesise information both within and between sources.
- For **full marks** candidates must refer to all sources in their answer.

'Objectivity' questions
- For **full marks** candidates must make an overall judgement as to the extent of the accuracy of the given statement. Maximum 6 marks if no overall judgement is made on extent of accuracy of the statement.
- Credit may be given up to **2 marks** for answers which evaluate the usefulness or reliability of the source; however this is not required for **full marks**.

'Conclusions' questions
- For **full marks** candidates must make conclusions/ judgements based upon evidence relating to the specific prompts in the question.
- Candidates are also required to make an overall conclusion about the issue in the question.

Higher Modern Studies marking grid for 12 marks questions (KU = 8 marks; analysis/evaluation = 4 marks)

	1 mark	2 marks	3 marks	4 marks
Range of relevant knowledge Accurate, relevant, up-to-date	One relevant aspect of the issue given with some description	Two relevant aspects of the issue given with some description or one relevant aspect covered with detailed and accurate description	One relevant aspect of issue with detailed and accurate description **and** one relevant aspect with some description	At least two relevant aspects with detailed and accurate descriptions – these should include the key aspects of the issue
Quality of explanation/ exemplification of knowledge Up to a maximum of **8 marks** available for knowledge and understanding	Some explanation of one aspect of the issue **or** relevant exemplification	Some explanation of two relevant aspects of the issue **or** detailed explanation of one aspect of the question which may include relevant exemplification	Detailed explanation of one relevant aspect of the issue with relevant exemplification **and** some explanation of one aspect of the question	At least two aspects of the question, fully explained, which relate closely to the key aspects of the question **and** extended, relevant, accurate and up-to-date exemplification
Analysis/evaluation Comments that identify relationships/ implications/make judgements **4 marks***	One relevant and accurate analytical or evaluative comment	One relevant and accurate analytical or evaluative comment that is justified **or** exemplified **or** two different relevant and accurate analytical/evaluative comments	One developed relevant and accurate analytical or evaluative comment that is justified **and** exemplified – this should relate closely to a key aspect of the question	One extended, accurate and justified analytical or evaluative comment of an insightful nature which relates closely to the key aspects of the question and is exemplified

*Where a candidate makes more analytical/evaluative points than are required to gain the maximum allocation of **4 marks**, these can be credited as knowledge and understanding marks provided they meet the criteria for this.

Answers to **12 marks** questions should demonstrate at least two relevant aspects of knowledge.

For **full marks** (12/12), a response must include a range of points, have detailed description/explanation, include a range of accurate exemplification and analysis or evaluation.

For **full marks** in the KU aspect of the question (8 marks), a response **must** include a range of points, have detailed explanation, and include accurate exemplification. Maximum of **6 marks** available (from 8 for KU) if there is no accurate or relevant exemplification.

Higher Modern Studies marking grid for 20 marks questions (KU = 8 marks; analysis/evaluation = 12 marks)

	1 mark	2 marks	3 marks	4 marks	5–6 marks
Range of relevant knowledge Accurate, relevant, up-to-date	One relevant aspect of the issue given with some description	Two relevant aspects of the issue given with some description **or** one relevant aspect covered with detailed and accurate description	One relevant aspect of the issue with detailed and accurate description **and** one relevant aspect with some description	At least two relevant aspects with detailed and accurate descriptions — these should include the key aspects of the issue	
Quality of explanation/ exemplification of knowledge Up to a maximum of **8 marks** available for knowledge and understanding	Some explanation of one aspect of the issue or relevant exemplification	Some explanation of two relevant aspects of the issue **or** detailed explanation of one aspect of the question which may include relevant exemplification	Detailed explanation of one relevant aspect of the issue with relevant exemplification **and** some explanation of one aspect of the question	At least two aspects of the question, fully explained, which relate closely to the key aspects of the question **and** extended, relevant, accurate and up-to-date exemplification	
Analysis Comments that identify relationships/implications, explore different views or establish consequences/ implications Up to **6 marks***	One relevant and accurate analytical comment	One relevant and accurate analytical comment that is justified **or** exemplified **or** two different relevant and accurate analytical comments	One developed relevant and accurate analytical comment that is justified **and** exemplified: this should relate closely to a key aspect of the question	One extended, accurate and justified analytical comment of an insightful nature which relates closely to the key aspects of the question and is exemplified	At least two developed relevant and accurate analytical comments that are justified **and** exemplified. These should relate closely to the question and may be linked for **6 marks**
Structure Structure which develops a consistent and clear line of argument Up to **2 marks**	Clear structure that addresses the issue identified in the question	Structure that clarifies the issue, presents evidence and develops a clear and consistent line of argument			
Conclusions Evaluative comments which make a judgement(s) and or reach a conclusion(s) which address the key issues in the question Up to **4 marks***	One conclusion that addresses a key issue in the question	One extended and balanced conclusion that addresses a key issue in the question **or** two conclusions that address key issues in the question	One extended and balanced conclusion that is justified and directly addresses the key issue(s) in the question **or** two balanced conclusions that address the key issues in the question, one of which is extended	One extended and balanced insightful conclusion that is justified and directly addresses the central aspects of the question **and** which considers a range of viewpoints	

*Where a candidate makes more analytical/evaluative points than are required to gain the maximum allocation of **4 marks**, these can be credited as knowledge and understanding marks provided they meet the criteria for this.

Answers to **20 marks** questions should demonstrate at least two relevant aspects of knowledge and provide detailed analysis and evaluation. For **full marks** in the KU aspect of the question (8/8), a response must include a range of points, have detailed explanation, and include a range of accurate exemplification.

Maximum of **6 marks** available (from 8 for KU) if there is no exemplification.

For **full marks** (20/20), a response must be structured, include a range of points, have detailed explanation, include a range of accurate and relevant exemplification and contain extended analysis and evaluation.

Higher Modern Studies marking grid for 8 marks source-based (objectivity/conclusions) questions

	1 mark	2 marks	3 marks	4 marks	5 marks	6 marks
Use of sources of evidence Up to **6 marks** available	One relevant piece of evidence relating to one aspect of the issue is used from one source	Two distinct pieces of evidence relating to one aspect of the issue which may be from within a single source or between sources	Two distinct pieces of evidence relating to one aspect of the issue are synthesised which may be from within a single source or between sources and an evaluative commentary is given	In addition; a second aspect of the issue is addressed with reference to one relevant piece of evidence	In addition; a second aspect of the issue is addressed with reference to linked evidence	In addition; a second aspect of the issue is addressed with reference to synthesised evidence including an evaluative commentary
Objectivity Analysis of the accuracy/selectivity/objectivity of a given view against evidence is presented Up to **2 marks** available	An objective assessment of a given view is stated, based on evidence presented from the sources	A detailed objective assessment of a given view is stated, based on evidence presented from the sources	1. For **full marks** candidates **must** refer to all sources in their answer. A maximum of **6 marks** if all sources are not used. 2. **Objectivity questions.** (i) Up to **6 marks** are available for the accurate evaluation of the given view using evidence. (ii) Candidates may also be credited up to **2 marks** on any comment/analysis of the origin and reliability of the sources. (iii) Up to **2 marks** are available for an overall judgement as to the extent of accuracy/objectivity of the view. 3. **Conclusions questions.** For **full marks** candidates must make evaluative comments/judgement(s)/ draw a conclusion about each of the points given in the question. **2 further marks** are available for an overall summative conclusion.			
Conclusionso Overall evaluative comment(s) derived from a judgement of the evidence presented Up to **2 marks** available	Overall conclusion is clear and supported by evidence from the sources	Overall conclusion is insightful and supported by detailed evidence from the sources				

HIGHER MODERN STUDIES
2014 SPECIMEN QUESTION PAPER

Section 1 — Democracy in Scotland and the United Kingdom

Question	General marking principles	Max marks	Detailed Marking Instructions for this question
1.	The candidate is required to interpret/evaluate up to three complex sources of information detecting and explaining the extent of objectivity. In order to achieve credit candidates must show evidence which supports the extent of accuracy in a given viewpoint. • Award up to **3 marks** for appropriate use of evidence depending on the quality of the explanation and the synthesis of the evidence for any one explanation of the extent of objectivity. • For **full marks** candidates must refer to all sources in their answer. • For **full marks** candidates must make an overall judgement as to the extent of the accuracy of the given statement. • Maximum of **6 marks** if no overall judgement made on extent of accuracy of the statement. • Candidates may be awarded up to a maximum of **2 marks** for incorporating an evaluation of the reliability of the sources in their explanations, although this is not mandatory.	8	*Candidates can be credited in a number of ways up to a maximum of 8 marks.* **Evidence that supports the view** (*… the televised debates had a significant impact on voting intentions*) • The televised debates allowed voters to visually connect with candidates *(1 mark)*. • Ipsos MORI poll revealed 60% of voters felt the debates would help them decide who to vote for. *Link to Source 2 — before first live debate 14% of voters indicated they would not vote for the main parties; following the leaders' initial performances this had decreased to 8% with the main parties receiving a boost in percentages of voters who would vote for them (2 marks).* • Coverage of the leaders during the debates could alter how the media reports on each of the leaders and their parties *(1 mark)*. • Success of TV debates increased Nick Clegg's popularity as a potential leader. *Link to Source 2 — 21% of voters claimed they would vote Liberal Democrat which rose to 32% following his performance during the first debate (2 marks).* • Following the debates, an independent polling organisation found over a million voters (4% of voters) altered the way they would vote. *Link to Source 2 — before the first debate Conservatives had a 5-point lead which disappeared following the leader's first performance (2 marks).* • TV debates motivated people to vote who may not have voted previously, with 17% rise in young voters indicating they would turn out to vote in some areas *(1 mark)*. **Evidence that does not support the view** (*…the televised debates had a significant impact on voting intentions*) • Only 12% said the survey changed their minds about who to vote for. *Link to Source 2 — very little change in percentages for Labour and Conservatives of voters who claimed they would vote for them in a General Election (2 marks).* • Source 1 — Initial viewing figures of 61% declined across the three debates *(1 mark)*. • Source 2 — Labour and Conservative vote remained largely unchanged *(1 mark)*. Candidates may also be credited up to **2 marks** on any comment/evaluation of the origin and reliability of the sources. • Source A — "Various" sources — extent of adaptation not known. Source therefore not wholly reliable • Comment on reliability of statistics from Ipsos MORI (both sources) • Reliability of statistics from British Election Study 2010 — well-respected organisation

Question		General marking principles	Max marks	Detailed Marking Instructions for this question
1.		(continued)		• Independent company survey — no reference to size of sample for survey, limited information on connection of company to TV debates; however, independent therefore may be less likely to be biased • Source B — full reference, including date; widely respected polling organisation — more reliable. For **full marks**, candidates **must** make an overall judgement as to the extent of the accuracy of the given statement. Overall, the evidence **does not** support view as: • *Source 1 — Liberal Democrats came third with only 23% of the vote (up only 1% from 2005) despite appearing to do best in the debates.* • *Source 2 — actual election results very close to statistics in first pie chart taken before televised debates.*
2.	(a)	Evaluation involves making a judgement(s) based on criteria, drawing conclusions on the extent to which a view is supported by the evidence; counter-arguments including possible alternative interpretations; the overall impact/significance of the factors when taken together; the relative importance of factors in relation to the context. Credit responses that make reference to: • the main features of an electoral system • an evaluation of the success of the electoral system in providing for fair representation Up to **8 marks** for KU (description, explanation and exemplification) and up to **4 marks** for evaluative comments. Award up to **6 marks** per point. Candidates should be credited up to **full marks** if they answer within a Scottish context only, a UK context only or refer to both Scotland and the UK. Where a candidate makes more evaluative points than are required to gain the maximum allocation of **4 marks**, these can be credited as knowledge and understanding marks provided they meet the criteria for this.	12	*Candidates can be credited in a number of ways up to a maximum of 12 marks.* **Credit reference to aspects of the following:** *Additional Member System:* • more opportunity to choose female or ethnic-minority candidates to increase representation • degree of proportionality allows for a wider range of parties to be featured in the Scottish Parliament which will benefit decision-making • number of votes gives voters a range of representatives from different parties with whom to discuss issues • increased accountability of representatives to voters • greater proportion of voters likely to get policy implemented that they voted for *Balanced by:* • impact of minority/majority government • impact of a coalition government, not directly voted for by voters • could be confusing for voters which may lead to a lower than normal turnout *First Past the Post:* • easy to understand and use in practice which could encourage turnout • direct link between MP and voters which increases accountability • usually produces a majority government which is able to drive through legislation in the interest of voters *Balanced by:* • tends to produce a two-party system: parliament has been dominated by two main parties in the post-war era — Labour and Conservative • impact of safe/marginal seats • no proportionality between votes and seats in some instances • government is often formed which is not reflective of voter choice • outdated electoral system as some parts of UK now have their own parliament as a result of devolution • it encourages tactical voting, as voters vote not for the candidate they most prefer, but against the candidate they most dislike *Any other valid point that meets the criteria described in the general marking principles for this type of question.*

Question		General marking principles	Max marks	Detailed Marking Instructions for this question
2.	(a)	(continued)		**Possible approaches to answering the question:** *Within the UK, a number of electoral systems are used to elect representatives to different parliaments. The Scottish Parliament uses the Additional Member System (AMS) to elect 129 MSPs and the UK Parliament uses First Past the Post (FPTP) to elect 650 MPs **(1 mark KU)**. The system used to elect the Scottish Parliament is said to provide better representation as voters get two votes whereas under FPTP they receive only one **(1 mark evaluative comment)**.* **(2 marks, one relevant point with limited description plus an evaluative comment)**
				*It could be said that AMS provides better representation as voters have two votes which allows for wider choice **(1 mark KU)**. Voters have one vote for a constituency MSP and one vote for a regional list MSP which could lead to a higher turnout if voters know their second vote helps elect a regional MSP from the party they support **(1 mark evaluative comment)**. Under FPTP, voters have only one choice for a constituency MP. This has led to the claim that many votes are 'wasted' because with FPTP, only votes to the winning candidate count. Second-placed candidates get nothing **(1 mark evaluative comment)**.* **(3 marks, one relevant point with a developed explanation plus evaluative comment)**
				*Systems of proportional representation are said to be fairer and provide for better representation amongst voters and the type of government which they result in. Since devolution, Scotland has used AMS to elect the 129 MSPs, a mixture of FPTP to elect constituency MSPs and regional list to elect 'top up' MSPs **(1 mark KU)**. The fact that voters have more choice and can choose between candidates both within and between parties reduces the need for tactical voting and provides for better representation **(1 mark evaluative comment)**. It could be said that FPTP which is used to elect the 650 MPs to Westminster most often produces a clear result as voters have one clear vote for the candidate of their choice; however on occasion this has led to governments being formed with less than half the votes which is not representative of voter choice **(1 mark KU, 1 mark evaluative comment)**. In 2010, the Conservatives gained 36.1% of the vote, failing to reach the 326 majority needed to form a government, resulting in a coalition with the Liberal Democrats who achieved 23% of the vote. Many would argue this outcome is not reflective of their votes **(1 mark KU, 1 mark evaluative comment)**.* **(6 marks, one relevant point with a fully developed explanation and a range of accurate, up-to-date exemplification plus relevant extended, evaluative comment)**

Question		General marking principles	Max marks	Detailed Marking Instructions for this question
2.	(a)	(continued)		*AMS is the system used to elect the Scottish Parliament. AMS is a form of proportional representation which is said to be fairer as it allows for wider representation compared to FPTP where the candidate with the most votes wins a seat in parliament and the party with the most MPs therefore becomes the government (**1 mark KU**). Under AMS there is more often wider representation as it allows smaller political parties such as the Liberal Democrats and Green Party to gain representation (**1 mark KU**). Under FPTP it tends to be the larger parties of Labour and Conservative which dominate government and which are more likely to hold an overall majority (**1 mark analysis**).* **(3 marks, two relevant points made with some explanation, a relevant example and limited evaluative comment)**
				*FPTP is used to elect MPs to the UK Parliament and the party with the most MPs forms the UK government. In a constituency the person with the most votes wins but the winner does not need the majority of the vote. This is also true of the government (**1 mark KU**). Since opening, the Scottish Parliament has used a form of proportional representation to elect MSPs called AMS. AMS is more proportional and means voters are more likely to get a candidate who they feel best represents them as the votes are distributed proportionally (**1 mark KU**). AMS has been better for smaller parties such as the Liberal Democrats who do better under AMS than they would under FPTP (**1 mark KU**). However, AMS more often leads to coalition politics which could affect decision-making. FPTP is more likely to produce a single party with a majority (**1 mark evaluative comment**).* **(4 marks, two relevant points, a relevant example plus a limited evaluative comment)**
				*Overall, it could be argued that AMS does provide fair representation as more often than not there are representatives from a range of political parties in the Scottish Parliament and, apart from the election in 2011, different parties have had to work together to run the country and make laws (**1 mark analysis**).* **(1 mark, overall evaluative comment that addresses the question)**
	(b)	Evaluation involves making a judgement based on criteria, drawing conclusions on the extent to which a view is supported by the evidence; counter-arguments including possible alternative interpretations; the overall impact/significance of the factors when taken together; the relative importance of factors in relation to the context.	12	*Candidates can be credited in a number of ways **up to a maximum of 12 marks.*** **Credit reference to aspects of the following (Scottish dimension):** • work of committees • questions to ministers • voting • Decision Time • debates and motions • impact of a majority/minority government • role and power of the whips • patronage power of the First Minister *Any other valid point that meets the criteria described in the general marking principles for this type of question.*

Question		General marking principles	Max marks	Detailed Marking Instructions for this question
2.	(b)	(continued) Credit responses that make reference to: • opportunities for parliamentary representatives to hold government to account • an evaluation of the effectiveness of parliamentary representatives in holding government to account Up to **8 marks** for KU (description, explanation and exemplification) and up to **4 marks** for evaluative comments. Award up to **6 marks** per point. Candidates should be credited up to **full marks** if they answer within a Scottish context only, a UK context only or refer to both Scotland and the UK. Where a candidate makes more evaluative points than are required to gain the maximum allocation of **4 marks**, these can be credited as knowledge and understanding marks provided they meet the criteria for this.		**Possible approaches to answering the question (Scottish dimension):** *There are many ways in which MSPs can hold the Scottish government to account such as asking a question at First Minister's Question Time (FMQT) which takes place every Thursday. During FMQT MSPs have the opportunity to ask questions of the First Minister in the debating chamber (1 mark).* **(1 mark, one relevant point made with an explanation)** *MSPs have a number of days in which they are able to hold the Scottish government to account. MSPs are able to submit a question to the presiding officer who will select six questions each week to be asked at FMQT which is every Thursday, lasting 30 minutes (1 mark KU). FMQT allows individual MSPs the opportunity to answer subject-specific questions and general questions. In November 2012, First Minister Alex Salmond was asked about his figures for further education funding and was forced to apologise over misleading parliament with inaccurate information (1 mark KU). Although not all questions are able to be asked, some MSPs may receive a written answer to their question instead (1 mark evaluative comment).* **(3 marks, one relevant point with a fully developed explanation and accurate, up-to-date and relevant exemplification plus limited evaluative comment)** *One of the founding key principles of the Scottish Parliament when it opened in 1999 was accountability. The Scottish Parliament has a number of procedures in place to ensure this principle is met including ministers and FMQT which allows MSPs to regularly hold government to account (1 mark KU). The First Minister is required to answer questions for 30 minutes every Thursday. On a number of occasions MSPs have posed questions to Alex Salmond about his government's actions. Depending on whether it is a minority or majority government this will have varying success (1 mark evaluative comment). The SNP currently has a majority government which puts opposition at a disadvantage. However there are occasions where FMQT has proved effective. In November 2012, Alex Salmond was forced to apologise to MSPs for misleading them with claims that an independent Scotland would have automatic claims to EU membership following reports the SNP had sought legal advice which later proved to be inaccurate (1 mark KU, 1 mark evaluative comment).* **(4 marks, one relevant point with a fully developed explanation and a range of accurate, up-to-date exemplification plus extended, qualified, evaluative comment)** *MSPs can influence the Scottish government and hold it to account in a number of ways. This can be done during FMQT, debates and discussions on proposed legislation such as the abolition of bridge tolls, and in committee work such as the Health Committee debating minimum alcohol pricing. MSPs can also vote on proposed laws (2 marks KU). However, there must be a majority of MSPs in favour of a law before it can be passed. For example, all parties except Labour were in favour of the proposed Alcohol (Minimum Pricing) Bill (1 mark evaluative comment).* **(3 marks, two relevant points with accurate and up-to-date exemplification plus relevant evaluative comment)**

Question		General marking principles	Max marks	Detailed Marking Instructions for this question
2.	(b)	(continued)		*Members of the Scottish Parliament can be very effective in holding the Scottish government to account. For example, there are a number of opportunities for MSPs to raise and debate issues, eg in parliamentary committees **(1 mark KU)**. Committees are made up of cross-party MSPs and they meet weekly or fortnightly to closely examine new laws or important Scottish issues **(1 mark KU)**. However, as the current Scottish government is a majority government, this means the SNP dominates most of the committees, such as the Health and Sports Committee, although this is chaired by a Labour MSP **(1 mark evaluative comment)**.*
				(3 marks, one relevant point with a fully developed explanation and accurate, up-to-date exemplification plus evaluative comment)
				In conclusion, MSPs can and do hold the Scottish government to account even if there is a majority government. The rules and procedures within the Scottish Parliament ensure all MSPs have the right to ask questions, be involved in committees and vote for and against legislation. Accountability is a key feature of the way in which the Scottish Parliament operates.
				(2 marks, overall detailed evaluative comment that addresses the question)
				Credit reference to aspects of the following (UK dimension): • debates • ministerial Question Time/Prime Minister's Question Time • voting • work of committees • impact of government majority/coalition • whip system • delaying power of House of Lords • motions of confidence
				Any other valid point that meets the criteria described in the general marking principles for this type of question.
				Possible approaches to answering the question (UK dimension): *There are many ways in which MPs in Parliament can hold the government to account. One way MPs can influence government is through the work of committees. There are a number of committees which meet in Parliament weekly to look at and discuss policies from each of the different departments, eg Health, Education, Transport and Environment **(1 mark KU)**.*
				(1 mark, one relevant point explained)
				*There are numerous ways in which Members of Parliament can hold the government to account. One of the most effective ways is select committees. One role of a select committee is to scrutinise the work of government departments **(1 mark KU)**. For example, the Health Committee recently met to discuss the role of the NHS at local level **(1 mark KU)**. Committees include a number of MPs from different political parties and they can be very effective in holding government to account. For example, Chancellor George Osborne was questioned by the Treasury Committee in 2011 over claims the 'windfall tax' could damage investment by the oil industry **(1 mark evaluative comment)**.*
				(3 marks, one relevant point explained, with an example and an evaluative comment)

Question		General marking principles	Max marks	Detailed Marking Instructions for this question
2.	(b)	(continued)		*Much of the work in the House of Commons and the House of Lords in holding the government to account is done through the work of committees. As a cross-party body, they have a minimum of 11 members whose job it is to examine issues in detail, including spending, government policy and proposed legislation. There are currently 19 committees in Westminster which gather evidence and make recommendations to the House of Commons based on their findings* **(2 marks KU)**. *However, government is under no obligation to act upon recommendations made and may reject them after a period of 60 days. It could be argued the work of committees is limited in holding government to account* **(1 mark evaluative comment)**. *Since 2010, however, the work of select committees has been strengthened by changes which now allow backbencher MPs to decide who represents the party and committee chairs are elected by secret ballot, which is arguably fairer than appointing committee members who are party loyalists* **(1 mark evaluative comment)**. *In January 2013, the Liaison Committee published a report re-examining the relationship between Parliament and government in light of the rising profile committees have played during investigations into claims of phone hacking, suggesting a 'growing role' for the committees. However this proposal was not accepted by government, highlighting that their work in holding the government to account is often limited* **(1 mark KU, 1 mark evaluative comment)**. **(6 marks, one relevant point with a fully developed explanation and a range of accurate and up-to-date exemplification plus relevant extended, qualified, evaluative comment)**
				MPs have the right to question ministers (Question Time) and the Prime Minister (PMQT) and government ministers in both the Commons and the Lords. On a Wednesday when the Commons is sitting the PM will spend half an hour answering questions **(1 mark KU)**. *However, there is never enough time to allow all MPs to ask questions with many critics claiming the PMQT is stage-managed and of little use in holding the government to account* **(1 mark evaluative comment)**. **(2 marks, one relevant point plus an evaluative comment)**
				There are occasions when backbench MPs can have great influence on the decision-making in central government. For example, it is Parliament and not the government of the day that makes the decisions and the laws so a majority of all MPs must vote in favour before a decision is made **(1 mark KU)**. *For example, MPs voted against UK military intervention in Syria and David Cameron had to accept the decision of Parliament* **(1 mark KU)**. *However, through the use of the party whip system, MPs are pressurised to vote according to the party's decision. The use of the party whip system, especially in a majority government, means there can be less of an effective check on the government* **(1 mark evaluative comment)**. **(3 marks, one relevant point, one example and one evaluative comment)**
				To finish, the UK government is effectively held to account especially through the use of committees which have real power. However, asking questions and voting are less effective as a way of holding government to account as a result of time and the whip system **(1 mark overall evaluative comment)**. **(1 mark overall evaluative comment that addresses the question)**

Section 2 — Social Issues in the United Kingdom

Question	General marking principles	Max marks	Detailed Marking Instructions for this question
1.	The candidate is required to interpret/ evaluate up to three complex sources in order to reach conclusions. In order to achieve credit candidates must show evidence which explains the conclusions reached. • Award up to **3 marks** for appropriate use of evidence depending on the quality of the explanation and the synthesis of the evidence to reach any one conclusion. • For **full marks** candidates must refer to all sources in their answer. • For **full marks** candidates must reach conclusions about each of the points given and make an overall conclusion on the issue.	8	*Links between social exclusion and health:* • *Health is poorer in people who are socially excluded. People who are socially excluded usually have higher death and illness rates (Source 1) **(1 mark)**.* • *Health is poorer in people who are socially excluded. People who are socially excluded usually have higher death and illness rates (Source 1). This is backed up in Source 3 where Glasgow has 22% of people with long-standing illness which is the highest of the four local authority areas **(2 marks)**.* • *Source 1 states the factors causing social exclusion are inter-related. Source 3 shows that the poorest local authorities — such as Dundee and Glasgow which have the highest unemployment rates (5.9% and 5.8% respectively) — have a range of poorer statistics such as higher long-standing illness rates (Glasgow 22% and Dundee 17%) and higher premature death rates — Dundee is 3rd and Glasgow highest (Source 2) **(3 marks)**.* *Links between social exclusion and local authority area:* • *Glasgow and Dundee have the highest premature death rates (Source 2) and this is backed up by Source 3 which shows Dundee and Glasgow have the highest unemployment rates **(1 mark)**.* • *Source 1 states that social exclusion is not equally spread across Scotland. This would be backed up by Source 3 which shows that Dundee (5.8%) and Glasgow (45%) have a higher percentage of the national share of the poorest parts of the country **(2 marks)**.* • *Source 1 states that social exclusion is not equally spread across Scotland and that there is a difference between urban and rural areas. This would be backed up by Source 3 which shows that Dundee (5.8%) and Glasgow (45%) have a higher percentage of the national share of the poorest parts of the country **(2 marks)**. There is further evidence in Source 2 to back this point up as Glasgow and Dundee have by far the highest levels of premature deaths, whereas more rural places such as Scottish Borders and Aberdeenshire have much lower premature death rates.* *Possible overall conclusions:* • *Overall, the evidence from each of the Sources 1–3 does suggest that social exclusion has a big impact in Scotland as it would appear that the poorest areas do have worse health and poorer social and economic data **(1 mark)**.* • *Overall, the evidence does suggest from Sources 1–3 that the factors that lead to social exclusion are strongly linked so that where social exclusion is greatest, health will be poorest. It is also clear that some parts of Scotland suffer more from social exclusion and these are also the local authority areas with the poorest social and economic data **(2 marks)**.*

Question		General marking principles	Max marks	Detailed Marking Instructions for this question
2.	(a)	An analysis mark should be awarded where a candidate uses their knowledge and understanding/a source to identify relevant components (eg of an idea, theory, argument, etc) and clearly show at least one of the following: • links between different components • links between component(s) and the whole • links between component(s) and related concepts • similarities and contradictions • consistency and inconsistency • different views/interpretations • possible consequences/implications • the relative importance of components • understanding of underlying order or structure Credit responses that make reference to: • government policies to tackle social inequalities • an analysis of policies with reference to a specific group Up to **8 marks** for KU (description, explanation and exemplification) and up to **4 marks** for analytical comments Award up to **6 marks** per point. Candidates may make reference to specific groups facing inequality on the basis of, for example: • gender • race • employment/unemployment • income/poverty • disability Candidates should be credited up to **full marks** if they answer within a Scottish context only, a UK context only or refer to both Scotland and the UK as appropriate. Where a candidate makes more analytical points than are required to gain the maximum allocation of **4 marks**, these can be credited as knowledge and understanding marks provided they meet the criteria for this.	12	**Credit reference to aspects of the following:** • details of the Equality Act 2012 • government policies, impact of the national minimum wage on female pay rates • gender pay gap, glass ceiling, over-representation in low-paid jobs, ie '5 Cs' (catering, cleaning, caring, clerical and cashiering) • impact of austerity measures, government cuts on welfare • reference to Equality and Human Rights Commission (EHRC) reports, Sex and Power Report, Joseph Rowntree Foundation (JRF) • rise in number of female-owned small businesses • women more likely to suffer poverty • credit also accurate references to other groups, eg ethnic minorities, people with disabilities, etc, and government policies to tackle inequalities *Any other valid point that meets the criteria described in the general marking principles for this type of question.* **Possible approaches to answering the question:** *Gender inequality exists in the UK. Men get paid more than women and women struggle to get the better-paid jobs. Government has introduced various policies to tackle these inequalities. These policies include the Equality Act 2010* **(2 marks KU).** <div align="right">**(2 marks, accurate point plus an example)**</div> *Gender inequality exists in the UK. Men's average earnings are higher (often around 15% and higher in best-paid employment) than women's and, for many types of jobs, women still experience a 'glass ceiling' that acts as a barrier to them obtaining the better-paid and more senior jobs, eg CEOs in big multinational companies* **(2 marks KU).** *Government has attempted to reduce some of these inequalities by introducing a variety of laws such as the Equality Act 2010. One part of the Equality Act is to ensure equal pay for equal work between men and women, although many groups such as Engender feel pay equality will take years to achieve* **(2 marks analysis).** *As well as tackling pay inequality, the Equality Act aims to get rid of gender discrimination. It is illegal to discriminate in employment on grounds of gender* **(1 mark KU).** *Nonetheless there have been several high-profile examples where women have won their cases on grounds of gender discrimination (eg in London City banking jobs)* **(1 mark KU).** *The reality is that many women feel the law is not strong enough and more needs to be done to end gender discrimination in employment. Recently one study claimed one in four women returning to work after maternity leave is the subject of discrimination* **(2 marks analysis).** <div align="right">**(8 marks, two separate accurate points, with description, explanation and exemplification plus extended analytical comment)**</div>

Question	General marking principles	Max marks	Detailed Marking Instructions for this question
(b)	An analysis mark should be awarded where a candidate uses their knowledge and understanding/a source to identify relevant components (eg of an idea, theory, argument, etc) and clearly show at least one of the following: • links between different components • links between component(s) and the whole • links between component(s) and related concepts • similarities and contradictions • consistency and inconsistency • different views/interpretations • possible consequences/implications • the relative importance of components • understanding of underlying order or structure Credit responses that make reference to: • lifestyle choices linked to poor health • an analysis of the consequences of specific lifestyle choices relating to poor health Up to **8 marks** for KU (description, explanation and exemplification) and up to **4 marks** for analytical comments. Award up to **6 marks** per point. Candidates should be credited up to **full marks** if they answer within a Scottish context only, a UK context only or refer to both Scotland and the UK as appropriate. Where a candidate makes more analytical points than are required to gain the maximum allocation of **4 marks**, these can be credited as knowledge and understanding marks provided they meet the criteria for this.	12	**Credit reference to aspects of the following:** • Poor lifestyle choices include smoking, excess alcohol consumption, lack of exercise, a diet high in salt and fat, drug misuse, or other risk-taking activities • Failure to make best use of preventative care services • Reference to government policies or health initiatives where it is acknowledged that these are a response to poor lifestyle choices, eg minimum alcohol pricing • Reference to official reports, eg Equally Well 2008 (and Inequalities Task Force Report 2010) • Statistical examples that highlight poor health in Scotland or the UK *Any other valid point that meets the criteria described in the general marking principles for this kind of question.* **Possible approaches to answering the question:** *Some people choose to drink too much alcohol. Scotland has a culture of binge drinking especially at the weekend which costs the country a great deal of money (1 mark KU).* **(1 mark, accurate and relevant point)** *Poor diet is a problem in Scottish society. Many people choose to eat too much fatty food such as burgers and chips. Too many people are now overweight or obese. Health campaigns such as the 5-a-day campaign to encourage people to eat more fruit and vegetables are a response to too many people choosing to eat a poor diet (2 marks KU).* **(2 marks, accurate point with an example)** *Despite years of anti-smoking health campaigns or the ban on smoking in public places, some individuals continue to choose to smoke cigarettes (1 mark KU). Around 22% of adults smoked in Scotland in 2012 (1 mark KU). As a consequence of smoking an individual is more likely to suffer from respiratory illness or lung cancer. Evidence shows that there is a strong link between smoking and lung cancer deaths. Around 90% of all lung cancer deaths are linked to people who smoked before they died (2 marks analysis).* **(4 marks, accurate point with explanation, exemplification and analysis)** *There are many lifestyle choices that can be made to improve health. For example, people can choose not to smoke, drink too much alcohol or eat too much fatty food (1 mark KU). Statistics show that Scotland has too many people who make the wrong lifestyle choices, eg around one in five adults smoke (1 mark KU). Choosing to take regular exercise is another important way that people can stay fit and healthy. Walking or cycling to school or work regularly has been proven to improve people's health. Unfortunately, not enough people in Scotland take regular exercise. Studies show that less than half the adult population takes an hour's exercise at least three times per week (2 marks KU). In Scotland the government has tried to encourage people to take more exercise by building cycle paths or by having subsidised entry to swimming pools or sports centres for children or people on a low income. The Equally Well Report of 2008 recognised that there was a need to promote exercise if Scotland was to further reduce the 'Big Three Killers' of heart disease, cancer and stroke (2 marks analysis).* **(6 marks, accurate developed point, with description, explanation, exemplification and extended analysis)**

Question	General marking principles	Max marks	Detailed Marking Instructions for this question
(c)	where a candidate uses their knowledge and understanding/a source to identify relevant components (eg of an idea, theory, argument, etc) and clearly show at least one of the following: • links between different components • links between component(s) and the whole • links between component(s) and related concepts • similarities and contradictions • consistency and inconsistency • different views/interpretations • possible consequences/implications • the relative importance of components • understanding of underlying order or structure Credit responses that make reference to: • government policies to tackle crime • an analysis of policies Up to **8 marks** for KU (description, explanation and exemplification) and up to **4 marks** for analytical comments. An analysis mark should be awarded Award up to **6 marks** per point. Candidates should be credited up to **full marks** if they answer within a Scottish context only, a UK context only or refer to both Scotland and the UK as appropriate. Where a candidate makes more analytical points than are required to gain the maximum allocation of **4 marks**, these can be credited as knowledge and understanding marks provided they meet the criteria for this.	12	**Credit reference to aspects of the following:** The Scottish government has introduced or extended a range of policies to reduce crime or improve crime prevention including: • policies to tackle antisocial behaviour • policies on counteracting the threat of terrorism • drugs — recovery and enforcement • new laws give greater protection to victims of forced marriage • tougher sanctions on crime linked to racial, religious or social prejudice • action on human trafficking • tough enforcement and prevention measures • protecting children from exploitation and dealing with extreme materials • policies on tackling prostitution and kerb-crawling offences • reducing re-offending • tackling serious organised crime in Scotland • reforming rape and sexual offences law • tackling misuse of firearms and air weapons in Scotland • youth justice measures — early intervention and tackling youth crime • introducing specialist drug courts • community payback orders • restriction of liberty orders Measures to implement some of the above were contained in the Criminal Justice and Licensing (Scotland) Act 2010. In England and Wales, the Home Office claims emphasis is moving towards local community-based approaches to reducing crime, including improving crime prevention: • creating community triggers to deal with persistent antisocial behaviour • using community safety partnerships, and police and crime commissioners, to work out local approaches to deal with issues, including antisocial behaviour, drug or alcohol misuse and re-offending • establishing the national referral mechanism (NRM) to make it easier for all the different agencies that could be involved in a trafficking case to co-operate, share information about potential victims and access advice, accommodation and support • setting up the National Crime Agency (NCA) which will be a new body of operational crime fighters • creating street-level crime maps to give the public up-to-date, accurate information on what is happening on their streets so they can challenge the police on performance • creating the child sex offender disclosure scheme, which allows anyone concerned about a child to find out if someone in their life has a record for child sexual offences • legislating against hate crime • using football banning orders to stop potential trouble-makers from travelling to football matches both at home and abroad • legislation to prohibit cash payments to buy scrap metal and reforming the regulation of the scrap metal industry to stop unscrupulous dealers buying stolen metal The Antisocial Behaviour, Crime and Policing Bill was announced in May 2013. It aims to tackle a number of types of crime including antisocial behaviour, illegal use of firearms and organised crime.

Question		General marking principles	Max marks	Detailed Marking Instructions for this question

2.	**(c)**	(continued)		References can be made to Scottish and/or UK-based crime reduction policies.
				
				Any other valid point that meets the criteria described in the general marking principles for this kind of question.
				
				Possible approaches to answering the question:
				To try and reduce crime in Scotland the Scottish government has announced it will increase the mandatory sentence for carrying a knife from four to five years. The Scottish government hopes this will stop young people carrying knives (1 mark KU).
				        (1 mark, accurate and relevant point)
				
				In Scotland there are many early intervention programmes that have been introduced to try and reduce crime. One early intervention programme is 'Kick It Kick Off' (KIKO) (1 mark KU). This programme uses football to try and steer young people, many who have had problems at school or with the police, away from trouble (1 mark KU). KIKO has been widely praised for its success in keeping many young people off the streets and out of trouble. KIKO programmes run in many parts of Scotland (1 mark analysis).
				    (3 marks, one accurate point explained with an example and analysis)
				
				The Criminal Justice and Licensing (Scotland) Act 2010 strengthened the law in terms of racial or religiously motivated crime. Now, where it has been proved that someone has committed an offence on grounds of race or religion (hate crimes), the courts must take this into account when handing out the sentence. This can lead to a longer custodial sentence or higher fine or a different type of punishment where appropriate (3 marks KU). Although many people support tougher punishments for hate crimes, arguing this will make some people think twice before committing a crime, there are those who believe longer or tougher sentencing is the wrong approach. These people would argue that there is little evidence tougher sentencing for hate crimes works (2 marks analysis).
				    (5 marks, one accurate developed point, with exemplification and extended analysis)

	(d)	An analysis mark should be awarded where a candidate uses their knowledge and understanding/a source to identify relevant components (eg of an idea, theory, argument, etc) and clearly show at least one of the following: • links between different components • links between component(s) and the whole • links between component(s) and related concepts • similarities and contradictions • consistency and inconsistency • different views/interpretations • possible consequences/implications • the relative importance of components • understanding of underlying order or structure Credit responses that make reference to: • a range of different crimes • an analysis of the consequences of crime for victims	12	**Credit reference to aspects of the following:** • reference to official crime figures or the Scottish Crime and Justice Survey, etc • range of types of crimes, eg violent and non-violent, and the short- and long-term effects of crime — physical, emotional, financial, psychological, etc • credit reference to crime where everyone is a victim in the widest sense, eg higher home/car insurance payments or more expensive prices when shopping • credit also references to the criminal justice system where again everyone in society is a victim in the widest sense • credit case studies and examples with reference to different crimes *Any other valid point that meets the criteria described in the general marking principles for this kind of question.* **Possible approaches to answering the question:** *To assault another person is a crime. This may result in a serious injury which requires medical attention (1 mark KU). Physically a person may be hurt after an attack but they may also be frightened. Some people do not go out as much if they have been the victim of an assault (1 mark analysis).* **(2 marks, accurate point explained plus analysis)**

Question		General marking principles	Max marks	Detailed Marking Instructions for this question
2.	(d)	(continued) Up to **8 marks** for KU (description, explanation and exemplification) and up to **4 marks** for analytical comments. Award up to **6 marks** per point. Candidates should be credited up to **full marks** if they answer within a Scottish context only, a UK context only or refer to both Scotland and the UK as appropriate. Where a candidate makes more analytical points than are required to gain the maximum allocation of **4 marks**, these can be credited as knowledge and understanding marks provided they meet the criteria for this.		*Someone who has their handbag stolen is the victim of a crime. The result may be that the person loses money, their mobile phone or other personal belongings* **(1 mark KU)**. *Theft or crimes of dishonesty were the most common type of crime in 2011–12 in Scotland, accounting for around half of all recorded crime.* **(1 mark KU)** *However, when someone has their handbag stolen they may also become the victim of other crimes such as identity fraud. In some cases, thieves will attempt to use credit cards to purchase goods on the internet, running up thousands of pounds of illegal purchases. Unfortunately, the victim, who has done no wrong, may find they have to spend weeks or even months sorting out their finances* **(2 marks analysis)**. **(4 marks, one accurate and exemplified point with 2 marks for more detailed analysis)** *Being a victim of burglary is a serious issue. Although burglaries as a type of crime are falling in Scotland, there are many consequences as a result of a burglary* **(1 mark KU)**. *The first consequence of a burglary is that people lose many of their household possessions such as laptops and jewellery, some of which may have personal value. Emotionally this can be very upsetting* **(1 mark analysis)**. *Another consequence of a burglary, this time financial, is that a person's house insurance may jump* **(1 mark analysis)**. *If a victim or the area a victim lives in suffers repeat burglaries then they may not be able to obtain affordable insurance, meaning if their house gets broken into again they may not be able to replace the goods they lose* **(1 mark KU)**. *There is also a cost to wider society from burglaries as the cost of insurance for the general population will rise* **(1 mark analysis)**. *Thanks to better police investigation techniques and improved house alarm and controlled entry systems, the number of burglaries is falling although it remains a more common type of non-violent crime* **(1 mark KU)**. **(6 marks, accurate developed point, with description, explanation, exemplification and extended analysis)**

Section 3 — International Issues

Question		General marking principles	Max marks	Detailed Marking Instructions for this question
1.	(a)	An analysis mark should be awarded where a candidate uses their knowledge and understanding/a source to identify relevant components (eg of an idea, theory, argument, etc) and clearly show at least one of the following: • links between different components • links between component(s) and the whole • links between component(s) and related concepts • similarities and contradictions • consistency and inconsistency • different views/interpretations • possible consequences/implications • the relative importance of components • understanding of underlying order or structure	20	**Credit reference to aspects of the following:** **The powers of the US president include:** • determine foreign policy and diplomacy • propose legislation • issue executive orders • submit the budget to Congress — but can refuse to release money for legislation that he/she disapproves of • adjourn/recall Congress at any time • make appointments • Commander in Chief of armed forces • negotiates treaties • veto **Limits on the US president by the Congress may include:** • may impeach the president (House of Representatives) • conducts the trial for impeachment (Senate) • 'filibuster' and delay legislation — this usually results in a forced compromise with the president • make it difficult/delay bills getting through Congress if there are divisions between Congress and the president or within their own party

Question		General marking principles	Max marks	Detailed Marking Instructions for this question
1.	(a)	(continued) Evaluation involves making a judgement based on criteria, drawing conclusions on the extent to which a view is supported by the evidence; counter-arguments including possible alternative interpretations; the overall impact/significance of the factors when taken together; the relative importance of factors in relation to the context. Credit responses that make reference to: • the political system in the world power • analysis of the ways the system checks government • balanced overall evaluative comment on the effectiveness of the political system in providing a check on government • provide a clear, coherent line of argument Up to **8 marks** for KU (description, explanation and exemplification) and up to **12 marks** for analytical/evaluative comments. Award up to **6 marks** per point. Candidates may make reference to any member of the G20 group of countries, excluding the United Kingdom. Where a candidate makes more analytical/evaluative points than are required to gain the maximum allocation of **4 marks**, these can be credited as knowledge and understanding marks provided they meet the criteria for this.		• Supreme Court recommendations must be approved by the Senate • many appointments subject to approval by US Senate • refuse to pass any laws during special sessions called by the president • Congress declares war and allocates money to fund it • Congress scrutinises any treaties and a 2/3 Senate majority is required to ratify them **Powers of the US Supreme Court which may include:** • declare executive orders unconstitutional (judicial review) Credit also: • powers of the states • role of the media • role of interest groups *Any other valid point that meets the criteria described in the general marking principles for this kind of question.* **Possible approaches to answering the question — World Power: China** • CPC is one-party state — no effective opposition • other political parties are not in opposition to CPC • treatment of political opponents • development of 'grassroots democracy' including town and village elections, 'independent candidates', 'focus groups', channels of communication, etc. • CPC controls the media • Hong Kong — 'One Country: Two Systems' — free media, opposition parties, etc, but half the HK government appointed by CPC *Any other valid point that meets the criteria described in the general marking principles for this kind of question.* **Possible approaches to answering the question — World Power: USA** *The president has the power to veto legislation. This means that even if a new law has been passed by Congress, the president can refuse to sign, sending the bill back to Congress unsigned. For example, President Bush vetoed a bill to allow stem cell research in 2007* **(2 marks KU).** **(2 marks, accurate point with an example)** *The president has the power to veto legislation. This means that even if a new law has been passed by Congress, the president can refuse to sign, sending the bill back to Congress unsigned. For example, President Bush vetoed a bill to allow stem cell research in 2007* **(2 marks KU).** *There are two types of presidential veto — the regular veto where during a session of Congress the president returns a bill unsigned, and the 'pocket veto'. If either type of veto happens legislation cannot proceed. This is one of the 'checks and balances' in the US political system* **(2 marks analytical comment).** **(4 marks, accurate point with explanation, exemplification and analytical/evaluative comment)**

Question		General marking principles	Max marks	Detailed Marking Instructions for this question
1.	**(a)**	(continued)		*The president has the power to veto legislation. This means that even if a new law has been passed by Congress, the president can refuse to sign, sending the bill back to Congress unsigned. For example, President Bush vetoed a bill to allow stem cell research in 2007 (2 marks KU). There are two types of presidential veto — the regular veto where during a session of Congress the president returns a bill unsigned, and the 'pocket veto'. If either type of veto happens legislation cannot proceed. The pocket veto occurs when Congress is adjourned and the president refuses to sign and the bill fails. By 2012, President Obama had twice used the pocket veto. This is one of the 'checks and balances' in the US political system (2 marks KU range of knowledge and 2 marks analytical comment). However, there are limits to the president's power to veto legislation. For example, if two-thirds of both Houses of Congress (Senate and Representatives) vote to override a presidential veto, the bill becomes law, eg the Medicare Bill was overridden by Congress in 2008. Then again, Congress can vote to override a presidential veto, causing the bill to become law without the president's approval, although this has rarely happened (2 marks evaluative comment).* **(8 marks, range of knowledge, description/explanation, exemplification and extended analytical/evaluative comment)** *Overall, there are many checks and balances within the US system of government that provide for an effective check on the government. The president may have many important powers such as control of the armed forces but Congress and on occasion the Supreme Court can check these powers. There is also the separation of powers between state governments and the federal government. This too ensures that no one part of government can become too powerful. The US Constitution defines clearly those powers that are given to states such as issuing licences (driving, firearms, etc), those that are shared and those that are given to the federal government. Taken as a whole, the US political system is very effective in checking the different parts of government (4 marks conclusions).* **(4 marks, balanced overall comment plus 2 marks for structure/line of argument)**
	(b)	An analysis mark should be awarded where a candidate uses their knowledge and understanding/a source to identify relevant components (eg of an idea, theory, argument, etc) and clearly show at least one of the following: • links between different components • links between component(s) and the whole • links between component(s) and related concepts • similarities and contradictions • consistency and inconsistency • different views/interpretations • possible consequences/implications • the relative importance of components • understanding of underlying order or structure	20	**Credit reference to aspects of the following:** **Possible approaches to answering the question — World Power: USA** • leading role as a permanent member of the UN Security Council • examples of US involvement in Afghanistan (ISAF) • leading role in NATO — examples of US involvement in Libya as part of Operation Unified Protector • possible future role of US in Syria • member of the G8 • largest economy in the world • role in Middle East • nuclear superpower • impact of emergence of China as superpower • withdrawal from Iraq/Afghanistan *Any other valid point that meets the criteria described in the general marking principles for this kind of question.*

Question		General marking principles	Max marks	Detailed Marking Instructions for this question
1.	(b)	Evaluation involves making a judgement based on criteria, drawing conclusions on the extent to which a view is supported by the evidence; counter-arguments including possible alternative interpretations; the overall impact/significance of the factors when taken together; the relative importance of factors in relation to the context. Credit responses that make reference to: • role/part played by world power in international relations • analysis of the importance of world power in international relations • balanced overall evaluative comment on the importance of the world power in international relations • provide a clear, coherent line of argument Up to **8 marks** for KU (description, explanation and exemplification) and up to **12 marks** for analytical/evaluative comments. Award up to **6 marks** per point. Candidates may make reference to any member of the G20 group of countries, excluding the United Kingdom. Where a candidate makes more analytical/evaluative points than are required to gain the maximum allocation of **4 marks**, these can be credited as knowledge and understanding marks provided they meet the criteria for this.		**Possible approaches to answering the question — World Power: China** **Credit reference to aspects of the following:** • leading role as a permanent member of the UN Security Council • participates in UN peace-keeping operations • relationship with and future role in negotiations with North Korea • impact of US/China diplomatic relations • investment in African countries and elsewhere • growing importance of China in world economy (2nd to the USA and expected to pass) • member of the G20 • part of the G8's Outreach Five (O5) *Any other valid point that meets the criteria described in the general marking principles for this kind of question.* **Possible approaches to answering the question — World Power: USA** *The USA's role as a world power is very important. It was one of the original countries that set up NATO in 1949 and still remains its most influential member. More recently the USA has played the lead role in NATO's mission to Afghanistan (ISAF) (2 marks KU).* <center>**(2 marks, accurate and exemplified but underdeveloped point)**</center> *The USA's role as a world power is very important. It was one of the original countries that set up NATO in 1949 and still remains its most influential member. More recently the USA has played the lead role in NATO's mission to Afghanistan (ISAF) (2 marks KU). In terms of finance, troop and resource commitments to NATO, the USA provides far more than any other single member of the Alliance, making the US the most important member of NATO, so in one sense the US can be seen as the most important member of the world's most powerful alliance (1 mark analysis).* <center>**(3 marks, accurate point with explanation, exemplification and analytical comment)**</center> *The USA's role as a world power is very important. It was one of the original countries that set up NATO in 1949 and remains its most influential member. More recently the USA has played the lead role in NATO's mission to Afghanistan (ISAF) (2 marks KU). In terms of finance, troop and resource commitments to NATO, the USA provides far more than any other single member of the Alliance, so in one sense the US can be seen as the most important member of the world's most powerful alliance (1 mark analysis). However, in recent years the USA has called on the other members of NATO to pay a greater share of the organisation's costs. The USA has also withdrawn a great many troops and resources from Europe in the expectation that European NATO members will do more for their own defence (1 mark analysis comment). Although the USA may dominate NATO in terms of its contribution, NATO's 28 members have equal standing, ie no one member country has more voting rights than the next and there must be agreement by all before action can be taken. This meant that for NATO to invade Afghanistan after 9/11, for example, all the members had to be in agreement (2 marks analysis/evaluative comment).* <center>**6 marks, accurate and developed point, exemplified with extended analytical/evaluative comment)**</center>
1.	(b)			

Question		General marking principles	Max marks	Detailed Marking Instructions for this question
1.	(b)	(continued)		*Therefore, given the importance of the USA within NATO, the UN, and the global economy, it is clear the USA is, at present, the world's most important country. For example, the US is sometimes described as 'the leader of the free world'. However, China is closing the gap in terms of the importance of the US to the world economy, as are the rest of the BRIC countries. Further, China has entered the space race and is increasing its influence in Africa. Also, despite US/NATO military strength in Afghanistan, the Taliban has not been defeated. The USA may be the world's only 'superpower' but this does not mean it has the power to achieve everything it seeks (4 marks conclusion).* (**4 marks, balanced overall comment**)
	(c)	An analysis mark should be awarded where a candidate uses their knowledge and understanding/a source to identify relevant components (eg of an idea, theory, argument, etc) and clearly show at least one of the following: • links between different components • links between component(s) and the whole • links between component(s) and related concepts • similarities and contradictions • consistency and inconsistency • different views/interpretations • possible consequences/implications • the relative importance of components • understanding of underlying order or structure Evaluation involves making a judgement based on criteria, drawing conclusions on the extent to which a view is supported by the evidence; the relative importance of factors; counter-arguments including possible alternative interpretations; the overall impact/ significance of the factors when taken together; the relative importance of factors in relation to the context. Credit responses that make reference to: • responses of international organisations to a significant world issue • analysis of the ways international organisations attempt to resolve a world issue • provide a clear, coherent line of argument Up to **8 marks** for KU (description, explanation and exemplification) and up to **12 marks** for analytical/ evaluative comments. Award up to **6 marks** per point Candidates may make reference to any world issue the impact of which extends beyond the boundaries of any single country. This impact may be regional or global in scale.	20	**Credit reference to aspects of the following:** • world issue: international terrorism (UN/NATO) • world issue: developing world poverty (UN agencies/ NGOs) • world issue: nuclear proliferation (UN) • world issue: global economic crisis (EU/World Bank/IMF) *Any other valid point that meets the criteria described in the general marking principles for this kind of question.* **Possible approaches to answering the question:** *The threat of the development of nuclear weapons by countries such as North Korea and Iran continues to be a major concern for the United Nations. As North Korea and Iran are not seen as stable democracies, it is a concern for the UN that either acquires nuclear capability (1 mark KU).* (**1 mark, accurate but underdeveloped point**) *The threat of the development of nuclear weapons by countries such as North Korea and Iran continues to be a major concern for the United Nations. The Treaty on the Non-Proliferation of Nuclear Weapons (updated 1995) was signed by 190 countries including North Korea. As North Korea and Iran are not seen as stable democracies, it is a concern for the UN that either acquires nuclear capability (2 marks KU). By way of response, the UN has imposed a variety of trade sanctions against North Korea and Iran. These sanctions aim to limit North Korea's ability to gain access to technology that would allow both countries to arm nuclear missiles. So far this policy seems to be partly working as it is claimed Iran has no nuclear weapons (2 marks analysis).* (**4 marks, accurate point with explanation, exemplification and analysis**)

Question		General marking principles	Max marks	Detailed Marking Instructions for this question
1.	(c)	(continued) Where a candidate makes more analytical/evaluative points than are required to gain the maximum allocation of **4 marks**, these can be credited as knowledge and understanding marks provided they meet the criteria for this.		*The threat of the development of nuclear weapons by countries such as North Korea and Iran continues to be a major concern for the United Nations. The Treaty on the Non-Proliferation of Nuclear Weapons (updated 1995) was signed by 190 countries including North Korea. As North Korea and Iran are not seen as stable democracies, it is a concern for the UN that either acquires nuclear capability* **(2 marks KU)**. *By way of response, the UN has imposed a variety of trade sanctions against North Korea and Iran. These sanctions aim to limit North Korea's ability to gain access to technology that would allow both countries to arm nuclear missiles. So far this policy seems to be partly working as it is claimed Iran has no nuclear weapons* **(2 marks analysis)**. *Despite these UN sanctions, the North Koreans continue to test or threaten to test nuclear weapons, increasing international tension. Recently, the North Koreans have talked of re-starting their nuclear programme to create nuclear material that could be used in weapons. They have also threatened to take action against South Korea and the USA which runs the risk of starting a devastating war. UN Secretary-General Ban Ki-moon has intervened to ask all sides to step back and, because of the seriousness of the situation, to think carefully about what they say* **(3 marks analytical/evaluative comment, 1 mark structure)**. **(8 marks, structure, description/explanation, exemplification and extended analytical/evaluative comment)** *Taken together, it can be argued that the United Nations has only been partly successful in attempting to limit the spread of nuclear weapons. Although around 200 countries signed up to the Treaty on the Non-Proliferation of Nuclear Weapons, and most countries of the world do not wish to develop nuclear weapons or share nuclear technology (some have even ended their interest in nuclear technology), more countries have become nuclear states or are suspected of having the capability to build or launch a nuclear missile. Unfortunately, the reality is that if some countries retain nuclear weapons then there will be others who will also want them* **(4 marks conclusion)**. **(4 marks, balanced overall comment)**
	(d)	An analysis mark should be awarded where a candidate uses their knowledge and understanding/a source to identify relevant components (eg of an idea, theory, argument, etc) and clearly show at least one of the following: • links between different components • links between component(s) and the whole • links between component(s) and related concepts • similarities and contradictions • consistency and inconsistency • different views/interpretations • possible consequences/implications • the relative importance of components • understanding of underlying order or structure	20	**Credit reference to aspects of the following:** • war — Afghanistan, Libya, Syria • nuclear weapons — North Korea • borders — Middle East • economic difficulties — EU countries (Portugal, Ireland, Italy, Greece, Spain) • factors which limit development *Any other valid point that meets the criteria described in the general marking instructions for this kind of question.* **Possible approaches to answering the question:** **Factors which affect development:** *One international issue is the lack of development in many countries in Africa. The lack of healthcare and education are said to be two of the most important factors limiting development* **(1 mark KU)**. **(1 mark accurate but underdeveloped point)**

Question		General marking principles	Max marks	Detailed Marking Instructions for this question
1.	(d)	(continued) Evaluation involves making a judgement based on criteria, drawing conclusions on the extent to which a view is supported by the evidence; the relative importance of factors; counter-arguments including possible alternative interpretations; the overall impact/significance of the factors when taken together; the relative importance of factors in relation to the context. Credit responses that make reference to: • explanation of the international issue • analysis of the impact of the issue in different countries • balanced overall evaluative comment on the extent to which an international issue has impacted on people in different countries • provide a clear, coherent line of argument Up to **8 marks** for KU (description, explanation and exemplification) and up to **12 marks** for analytical/evaluative comments. Award up to **6 marks** per point. Candidates may make reference to any world issue the impact of which extends beyond the boundaries of any single country. This impact may be regional or global in scale. Where a candidate makes more analytical/evaluative points than are required to gain the allocation of **4 marks**, these can be credited as knowledge and understanding marks provided they meet the criteria for this.		*One international issue is the lack of development in many countries in Africa. The lack of available and affordable healthcare and education are said to be two of the most important factors limiting development* **(1 mark KU).** *For example, in Malawi life expectancy is low (54 years) and illiteracy rates are high (one in six people cannot read or write)* **(1 mark KU).** *However, in recent years many African countries have seen real improvements in standards of living, many experiencing faster economic growth than countries in Europe* **(1 mark analytical comment).** *Free from civil war, the people of countries such as Mozambique and Angola have been able to invest in schools and medical clinics and have made progress in reducing illnesses such as HIV/AIDS or increasing the number of children in primary school* **(1 mark analysis, 1 mark KU).** **(5 marks, accurate point with explanation, exemplification and extended analysis/evaluative comment)** *Overall, development in African countries has been mixed if, for example, measured against the UN's Millennium Development Goals. Countries that have experienced good government and have been free from war, such as Tanzania and Ghana, have made sustained progress. However, where the government has been accused of corruption (Nigeria) or where there has been conflict (Sudan), there has been much less progress* **(3 marks conclusion).** **(3 marks, balanced overall comment)**

Section 1 — Democracy in Scotland and the United Kingdom

Question	General Marking Instructions for this type of question	Max marks	Specific Marking Instructions for this question
1. (a)	An analysis mark should be awarded where a candidate uses their knowledge and understanding/a source to identify relevant components (eg of an idea, theory, argument, etc) and clearly show at least one of the following: • links between different components • links between component(s) and the whole • links between component(s) and related concepts • similarities and contradictions • consistency and inconsistency • different views/interpretations • possible consequences/implications • the relative importance of components • understanding of underlying order or structure Evaluation involves making a judgement based on criteria, drawing conclusions on the extent to which a view is supported by the evidence; the relative importance of factors; counter-arguments including possible alternative interpretations; the overall impact/significance of the factors when taken together; the relative importance of factors in relation to the context. Credit responses that: • make reference to the political system in Scotland, the political system in the UK or the political system in Scotland and the UK • provide balanced evaluative comments referring to different factors and their relative importance/impact • provide a clear, coherent line of argument Up to **8 marks** for KU (description, explanation and exemplification) and up to **12 marks** for analytical/evaluative comments (4 of these marks specifically for conclusions). Award up to **6 marks** per point. Where a candidate makes more analytical/evaluative points than are required to gain the maximum allocation of 8 marks, these can be credited as knowledge and understanding marks provided they meet the criteria for this.	20	*To what extent are some factors more important than others in influencing voting behaviour?* *Candidates can be credited in a number of ways up to a maximum of 20 marks.* **Credit reference to aspects of the following:** • The different factors that influence voting behaviour • Implications of different factors influencing voting behaviour Answers may refer to: A range of factors that are said to affect voting behaviour including: • Media • Social Class • Age • Gender • Geographical location/Residence • Ethnicity • Party leader competence and Image • Issues Credit those candidates who integrate factors and highlight links between some factors, eg public perception of issues, party leader image and public awareness of party policy can be seen to be linked to media representation of these issues. Also, link between social class and occupation, education, income, etc. • Discussion of relative importance of different factors • De-alignment, long term/short term factors • Other relevant points *Any other valid point that meets the criteria described in the general marking instructions for this kind of question.* **Possible approaches to answering this questions:** **Response 1** • One factor that can affect how someone votes is the media. The media includes newspapers, television and radio as well as 'new media' such as social networking. The media plays an important role in how a leader or a political party and their policies are portrayed and parties such as the Labour Party, the Conservatives and the SNP clearly believe that the media plays a part in influencing how people vote as they spend a lot of money on spin doctors, media monitoring units and rapid rebuttal teams to ensure that the public are aware of their policies. This shows that the media can be a factor in influencing voting behaviour **(2 marks KU, 1 mark analysis)**. **Response 2** • The media is also important in informing and shaping public opinion about current issues affecting the nation. Issues that have affected how people voted in recent elections include immigration, the war in Iraq and the handling of the economy. For many voters, the state of the economy is a big factor in how they vote. If the economy is doing well and people are in work and can afford a decent standard of living, they are more likely to vote for the party in power. However, if the economy is doing badly, many voters are likely to blame the government and vote for other parties. For example, following the recession of 2008, many voters blamed the former Prime Minister Gordon Brown for the poor running of the economy. At the next election in 2010, the public voted to change the government. Many voters gave the poor economy as the reason for how they voted **(2 marks KU, 3 marks analysis)**.

Question	General Marking Instructions for this type of question	Max marks	Specific Marking Instructions for this question
1. (a)	(continued)		**Response 3** • Social class is an important factor which will affect the way a person votes. Society is divided into different classes depending on a person's status. It is defined based on occupation, income, education and home ownership. Classes are divided into A, B, C, D and E, with those in social class A and B usually in a professional occupation such as accountants or surgeons. Those in groups D or E would include the poorest who may be in unskilled work or unemployed. Historically election results have shown that those in A and B often support the Conservatives, whilst DE voters support Labour because Labour policies such as Tax Credits and the National Minimum Wage have benefitted the poorest. However class dealignment means that there is an increase in middle classes and so the role of social class is less influential. In 2010 40% of DE voters, voted Labour. Therefore social class is an important factor, but not as important as it used to be **(5 marks KU, 2 marks analysis).**
(b)	An analysis mark should be awarded where a candidate uses their knowledge and understanding/a source to identify relevant components (eg of an idea, theory, argument, etc) and clearly show at least one of the following: • links between different components • links between component(s) and the whole • links between component(s) and related concepts • similarities and contradictions • consistency and inconsistency • different views/interpretations • possible consequences/implications • the relative importance of components • understanding of underlying order or structure Evaluation involves making a judgement based on criteria, drawing conclusions on the extent to which a view is supported by the evidence; counter-arguments including possible alternative interpretations; the overall impact/significance of the factors when taken together; the relative importance of factors in relation to the context. Credit responses that: • make reference to the political system in Scotland, the political system in the UK or the political system in Scotland and the UK • provide balanced evaluative comments referring to the effectiveness of different forms of participation and their relative importance/impact • provide a clear, coherent line of argument	20	*Most citizens participate effectively in the political process.* *Discuss* *Candidates can be credited in a number of ways up to a maximum of 20 marks.* **Credit reference to aspects of the following:** • The various methods of participation in politics • The effectiveness of different types of participation Answers may refer to: The various methods of participation in politics: • Voting • Joining a party/campaigning • Pressure group membership/participation • Protest — various forms legal or illegal • Participation through interaction with the media • Standing for election at various levels **Possible approaches to answering the question:** **Response 1** • UK citizens can participate simply by voting for representatives at various elections. An example of this would be the last UK General Election when almost 30 million citizens voted in 650 constituencies and returned a coalition government made up of MPs from the Liberal Democrats and Conservatives **(2 marks KU).** **Response 2** • Many Scottish people voted in the recent Independence referendum. The turnout for this referendum was almost 85%, an extremely high participation rate. Many scots believed it was their responsibility to participate in this way as the issue in question was so important. The high turnout added legitimacy to the eventual "No" result and shows that registering and participating was effective. This was the first time many Scots had actually registered to vote. Many argue that this increased participation has actually changed Scotland for good, making it a more democratic country **(1 mark KU — 1 mark analysis, 1 mark evaluation).**

Question		General Marking Instructions for this type of question	Max marks	Specific Marking Instructions for this question
1.	(b)	(continued) Up to **8 marks** for KU (description, explanation and exemplification) and up to **12 marks** for analytical/evaluative comments. Award up to **6 marks** per point. Where a candidate makes more analytical/evaluative points than are required to gain the maximum allocation of **4 marks**, these can be credited as knowledge and understanding marks provided they meet the criteria for this.		**Response 3** • Many citizens take part in pressure group activity in the UK. Some groups (insider groups such as the CBI) are effective in their activities and have close links to government. However, some "outsider groups" are less successful in their campaigns as they are seen as being hostile to government and are often demanding radical changes. A group such as Greenpeace has many thousands of members who are participating in the political process through their membership but their activities are often unsuccessful in changing government environmental policy. Groups like this have often taken part in activities which may be illegal thus reducing their effectiveness in winning over public and government opinion. Many citizens do participate in the political process, but not all are effective **(3 marks KU, 2 marks analysis, 1 mark evaluation)**. **Response 4** • Most UK citizens do not participate in any effective way in the political process. Many never vote in any election. Turnouts at local council elections and European elections often fall below 30%. Many others do vote but due to the electoral system, especially in Westminster elections, their votes are ineffective as they support a candidate from a minor party such as the Greens who have little chance of winning their constituency or forming the government. Participation is seen as ineffective by these people as they feel unable to influence the result **(2 marks KU, 2 marks evaluation)**. *Any other valid point that meets the criteria described in the general marking principles for this kind of question.*

Section 2 – Social Issues in the United Kingdom

Question		General Marking Instructions for this type of question	Max marks	Specific Marking Instructions for this question
2.		The candidate is required to interpret/evaluate up to three complex sources of information detecting and explaining the extent of objectivity. In order to achieve credit candidates must show evidence which supports the extent of accuracy in a given viewpoint. • Award up to 3 marks for appropriate use of evidence depending on the quality of the explanation and the synthesis of the evidence for any one explanation of the extent of objectivity. • For **full marks** candidates must refer to all sources in their answer. • For **full marks** candidates must make an overall judgment as to the extent of the accuracy of the given statement. • Maximum of 6 marks if no overall judgement made on extent of accuracy of the statement. • Candidates may be awarded up to a maximum of 2 marks for incorporating an evaluation of the reliability of the sources in their explanations although this is not mandatory.	8	*To what extent is it accurate to state that the government's anti-smoking policies are successfully tackling the problem of smoking in Scotland?* *Candidates can be credited in a number of ways **up to a maximum of 8 marks**.* **Evidence that supports the view ("the government's anti-smoking policies are successfully tackling the problem of smoking in Scotland?")** **Examples of the types of evidence that support the view include:** • Source A, 23% of adults smoke in Scotland, less than a quarter and a downward trend backed by Source B: 23% of all adults smoke. • Source C, smoking rates for all young people who are regular smokers are declining both boys and girls and predicted to remain steady. • Source C, 13yr old girls and boys are now virtually the same or lower than before. • Source C, 3 of the 4 groups shown have all declined since 2006 (all but 15yr old boys) link to smoking ban in Source A. • Source A: Only 10% of people living in the least deprived areas smoke. Link to Source B: levels below the average of 23% include those in full time employment 22% and those who are self-employed 22%. • Source A: Less than one quarter (23%) of adults smoked in 2013 which continues a general downwards trend in the proportion of adults who smoke. Link to Source C: this trend continues in young people as the number has decreased or remained steady.

Question	General Marking Instructions for this type of question	Max marks	Specific Marking Instructions for this question
2.	(continued)		• Source C, rates for young smokers have reduced dramatically since 1996 (30%) to around 15% in 2012, so the message is getting through.
			Response 1 The number of adults smoking is falling according to Source 1. This is backed by the downward trend in 13 and 15 year olds smoking as shown in Source C. This shows that since 2006 smoking has fallen amongst all groups, most especially among 15 year old girls. This figure has fallen by 5% since 2006. The smoking ban and increasing the age to buy cigarettes to 18 may have helped cause this, a clear success of policy **(3 marks, evidence synthesised from two sources with evaluative comment).**
			Evidence that opposes the view ("the government's anti-smoking policies are successfully tackling the problem of smoking in Scotland?")
			• Source A: Smoking is the main cause of early death. • Source A, cost to NHS remains high, £271m/yr. • Source A: 13,000 deaths per year where smoking is the main cause of death. • Source A: As many as 600 children take up smoking each day. Scotland has the highest rate behind England. • Source A: 39% of those in the most deprived areas in Scotland smoke, Link to Source B: deprived areas tend to high level so unemployment, 51% of adult unemployed and looking for work smoke, supported by link to Source A which states those out of work are most likely to smoke. • Source B: highest rate of adult smokers 60%, those who are unable to work due to short term illness, sick or disabled (51%) also links to Source A which states those out of work are most likely to smoke. • Source A: despite all previous attempts to reduce smoking among young people, age increased to 18yrs, restrictions on cigarette displays, 50 children a day start smoking in Scotland. • Source C, 15yr old girls continue to become regular smokers, 12%, this is higher than boys. Link to Source A: previous attempts to target smoking in young people. • Source A: Scottish Government continues to target smoking in its policy, trying to stop young people starting. • Scotland has the highest smoking rates in the UK, 23%.
			Response 2 The policies of the government are not successful in tackling smoking in Scotland as 23% of Scots still smoke which is the highest **(1 mark, one relevant piece of evidence from one source).**
			Candidates may also be credited up **to** 2 marks on any comment/analysis of the origin and reliability of the source. • Information from Source B is taken from the Scottish Government's website which has a responsibility to publish accurate and recent data for public information **(1 mark).** • Information from Source C is taken from ASH Scotland, is a well-known voluntary organisation that provides evidence based information on tobacco. However it may be seen as biased as it receives some of its funding from Scottish Government which is committed to cutting smoking rates **(2 marks).**

Question	General Marking Instructions for this type of question	Max marks	Specific Marking Instructions for this question
2.	(continued)		• The information in Source A is adapted from a BBC news article published online with additional information from Cancer Research UK. As the article has been adapted it may be less reliable than when originally written. Also it is not clear what parts come from exactly which source **(2 marks)**. • Statistics in Source A are up to date (2012, 2013) **(0 marks)**. • Statistics in Source A are up to date (2012, 2013) and so give a fairly up to date picture of the smoking issue **(1 mark)**. For **full marks**, candidates **must** make an overall judgment as to the extent of the accuracy of the given statement. Overall, the evidence **does** support the view as: • On the whole, the evidence suggests that smoking is being successfully tackled by the government's policies. The number of adults smoking is falling. It may still be higher in Scotland than in any other country in the UK but importantly the number of young smokers is falling rapidly as shown in Source C this is also backed by the extremely low number of schoolchildren smoking, only 3% **(2 marks)**. • The statement is mostly true as smoking is a declining problem as can be seen from Source C. There are still too many children starting to smoke so the government's policies may be slow, but they are working **(1 mark)**. The statement is partly true as fewer adults are smoking (23% and falling) possibly as a result of the smoking ban which was introduced in 2006. However, those who are unemployed or dependent on benefits have not been helped as is shown in Source B, over half of those in the three categories, Unemployed, Disabled and short term illness are smokers **(2 marks)**.

Part A: Social inequality in the UK

Question	General Marking Instructions for this type of question	Max marks	Specific Marking Instructions for this question
3. (a)	Evaluation involves making a judgement(s) based on criteria, drawing conclusions on the extent to which a view is supported by the evidence; counter-arguments including possible alternative interpretations; the overall impact/significance of the factors when taken together; the relative importance of factors in relation to the context. Up to **8 marks** for KU (description, explanation and exemplification) and up to **4 marks** for evaluative comments. Award up to **6 marks** per point. Candidates should be credited up to **full marks** if they answer within a Scottish context only, a UK context only or refer to both Scotland and the UK. Where a candidate makes more evaluative points than are required to gain the maximum allocation of **4 marks**, these can be credited as knowledge and understanding marks provided they meet the criteria for this.	12	*Evaluate the view that social inequality affects some groups in society more than others* *Candidates can be credited in a number of ways up to a maximum of 12 marks.* Credit responses that make reference to: • the nature of social inequality • socio-economic groups and the impact of inequalities on them • an evaluation of the importance of various socio-economic factors in causing inequality Credit reference to aspects of the following: • Age groups • Ethnicity • Gender • Class • Disability • Health Inequalities • Income Inequalities • Housing Inequalities • Education • Crime • Discrimination • Family structure • Poverty *Any other valid point that meets the criteria described in the general marking principles for this kind of question.* **Possible approaches to answering the question:** **Response 1** • Groups who do not do well in the education system may not find a job and so will be unemployed and have to rely on benefits **(1 mark KU).** **Response 2** • Women in the UK are more likely to be living in poverty. One reason may be that they are more likely to be the head of a single parent family. This creates obvious pressures on time and often results in welfare dependency for the family. Recent statistics show that around 90% of lone parent families are headed by a woman and over 25% of children now live with a lone mother **(2 marks KU).** **Response 3** • There are major inequalities in health affecting certain groups in the UK. Life expectancy among the poorest people in Scotland is much lower than among the richest. Within Glasgow, male life expectancy varies by as much as twenty seven years between the poorest and richest areas. Poor health certainly affects the poorest more as a result of lifestyle choices which are limited partly by low income. Poor diet and a lack of exercise are the main causes of health problems for our poorest groups. Many Scots choose to eat too much fatty food and healthy eating campaigns, such as the 5-a-day campaign, have had less impact on poorer areas where fresh fruit and vegetables are not only less easily available but are often too expensive. Such issues do not affect those on higher incomes who can afford fresh food and can travel more easily to a wider variety of shops. The poorest groups in society suffer greater ill health which leads to lower earnings, lower educational attainment etc ie multiple deprivation. As a result the poor will continue to suffer health inequalities **(3 marks KU, 2 marks evaluation).**

Question		General Marking Instructions for this type of question	Max marks	Specific Marking Instructions for this question
3.	(a)	(continued)		**Response 4** • Some people would question the link between poverty and social inequality. They would claim that many people have become successful even although they came from a poor community with few amenities and were not encouraged to succeed in education. For example, Brian Souter has become very wealthy through starting several transport companies. He is the son of a bus driver and certainly not from a wealthy background. However, although there may be cases of successful people from poor backgrounds evidence shows that people from wealthy middle class families are more likely to go to university and therefore more likely to have much higher lifetime earnings. Consequently, poor children are likely to grow up poor adults **(1 mark KU, 3 marks evaluation)**. *Any other valid point that meets the criteria described in the general marking principles for this kind of question.*
3.	(b)	Evaluation involves making a judgement(s) based on criteria, drawing conclusions on the extent to which a view is supported by the evidence; counter-arguments including possible alternative interpretations; the overall impact/significance of the factors when taken together; the relative importance of factors in relation to the context. Up to **8 marks** for KU (description, explanation and exemplification) and up to **4 marks** for evaluative comments. Award up to **6 marks** per point. Candidates should be credited up to **full marks** if they answer within a Scottish context only, a UK context only or refer to both Scotland and the UK. Where a candidate makes more evaluative point than are required to gain the maximum allocation of **4 marks**, these can be credited as knowledge and understanding marks provided they meet the criteria for this.	12	*Evaluate the effectiveness of <u>either</u> the benefits system <u>or</u> health services in tackling social inequality.* Credit responses that make reference to: • the role of the benefits system in tackling inequality • an evaluation of the success/shortcomings of the benefits system in tackling social inequality OR Credit responses that make reference to: • the role of health services (public and/or private) in tackling inequality • an evaluation of the success/shortcomings of health services in tackling social inequality *Candidates can be credited in a number of ways up to a maximum of 12 marks.* Possible approaches to answering the question: **Response 1** • UK citizens who have no other source of income or are on a low income are helped by a wide range of welfare benefits provided by central government. The old age pension, universal benefit and housing benefit are just three which try to meet the needs of many people **(2 marks KU)**. **Response 2** • Child benefit is paid to families who earn below a certain amount to help with the additional costs of bringing up children. The amount paid is £20.50 per week for the eldest child and £13.55 for each additional child. This helps to tackle inequality as these payments are very important to those who have a very low income and make a big difference to the family income in a poor household. Child benefit is not paid in full to households with a high income — after £50,000 the amount of child benefit paid is reduced. This means that it helps to reduce inequality as families on low income get more in benefit than high-income families **(2 marks KU, 1 mark evaluation)**.

Question		General Marking Instructions for this type of question	Max marks	Specific Marking Instructions for this question
3.	(b)	(continued)		**Response 3** • Critics would claim that the National Health Service is not effective in tackling inequality as it is under-staffed and under-funded. Recent media coverage has concentrated on the winter pressures faced by Accident and Emergency departments across the UK. Many of the departments have failed to meet targets set for them regarding waiting and discharge times. However, it could also be argued that as a society we expect so much from the NHS that it is almost certain to fail to meet these expectations. Despite its problems and failings the NHS has contributed hugely to tackling social inequality in the UK. Without its universal, free at the point of need principles then the majority of citizens would struggle to afford healthcare. Life expectancy and infant mortality figures have improved greatly for the poorest since the NHS was introduced. If we are to maintain these improvements then we will either have to reorganise the NHS, lower our expectations or be willing to pay more tax to fund it. Overall, the NHS has been vital in improving the living conditions in our society **(2 marks KU, 3 marks evaluation)**. **Response 4** • Many in the UK now rely on private health care as well as the government funded NHS. Over 15% of all that is spent on health care in the UK is spent by the private sector rather than by the NHS. This creates a divide in society and effectively makes inequality worse. Those who can afford to go private can skip the queue and those who can't have to wait for a poorer service from the NHS **(1 mark KU, 2 marks evaluation)**. *Any other valid point that meets the criteria described in the general marking principles for this kind of question.*

Part B: Crime and the law in the UK

Question		General Marking Instructions for this type of question	Max marks	Specific Marking Instructions for this question
3.	(c)	Evaluation involves making a judgement(s) based on criteria, drawing conclusions on the extent to which a view is supported by the evidence; counter-arguments including possible alternative interpretations; the overall impact/significance of the factors when taken together; the relative importance of factors in relation to the context. Up to **8 marks** for KU (description, explanation and exemplification) and up to **4 marks** for evaluative comments. Award up to **6 marks** per point. Candidates should be credited up to **full marks** if they answer within a Scottish context only, a UK context only or refer to both Scotland and the UK.	12	*Evaluate the view that crime only affects the victims.* Credit responses that make reference to: • the personal impact of crime on the individual • an evaluation of the relative impact of crime on family, community, wider society, economy, government etc Credit reference to aspects of the following: • likely victims — age, gender, race etc • physical impact • psychological impact • economic/financial impact • impact on families • impact on local community • impact on local business • impact on wider society • impact on offender • political/legal impact — eg new anti-terror legislation *Any other valid point that meets the criteria described in the general marking principles for this kind of question.* *Candidates can be credited in a number of ways **up to a maximum of 12 marks**.*

Question		General Marking Instructions for this type of question	Max marks	Specific Marking Instructions for this question
3.	(c)	(continued) Where a candidate makes more evaluative point than are required to gain the maximum allocation of 4 marks, these can be credited as knowledge and understanding marks provided they meet the criteria for this.		**Possible approaches to answering the question:** **Response 1** • Assaulting a person is a crime. The person may need to go to hospital as they have been injured. As well as a physical injury the crime may leave a psychological injury on the victim ie they may be scared to go out and have no confidence. The victim is affected in two ways **(1 mark KU, 1 mark evaluation)**. **Response 2** • It is not just the direct victim of a crime who is affected by it. There could also be an impact on their family. If the person is severely injured then they may be unable to return to work meaning a drop in income and all the difficulties this may bring eg poorer lifestyle, diet, health etc. In this way crime can affect a much wider group. The family of the offender may also be affected by the crime. They may feel ashamed and be shunned by their community. These are often more serious and longer lasting than the initial physical damage to the victim. It is too simplistic to say that only the "victim" is affected **(3 marks evaluation)**. **Response 3** • Often the whole community is affected by a criminal act. From the actions of only a very small group of offenders a local area can gain a "bad" reputation if there is too much violent crime. For example, some parts of Glasgow have a reputation for violent gang crime. This can have a negative effect on the spirit of the people who live there but can also have a negative effect on the area's economy. If people don't want to live there then house prices may drop. Household and car insurance in the area may become more expensive, further driving people away. People who stay will have less to spend. Local business may not wish to be associated with the area leading them to relocate. Unemployment may then rise further reducing the desirability of the area. Local business will of course suffer as they may have to pay higher insurance premiums etc. Overall, to suggest that crime only affects the victim is clearly wrong. It can have a negative impact on the social and economic life of an entire community. On the other hand the impact of a major crime could bring a community together and create a determination among people that the community will get over it and grow stronger. A good example of this was the midnight anti-rape protests which took place in Glasgow in order to support the victims and to show solidarity against criminals **(3 marks KU, 3 marks evaluation)**. *Any other valid point that meets the criteria described in the general marking principles for this kind of question.*

Question		General Marking Instructions for this type of question	Max marks	Specific Marking Instructions for this question
3.	(d)	Evaluation involves making a judgement(s) based on criteria, drawing conclusions on the extent to which a view is supported by the evidence; counter-arguments including possible alternative interpretations; the overall impact/significance of the factors when taken together; the relative importance of factors in relation to the context. Up to **8 marks** for KU (description, explanation and exemplification) and up to **4 marks** for evaluative comments. Award up to **6 marks** per point. Candidates should be credited up to **full marks** if they answer within a Scottish context only, a UK context only or refer to both Scotland and the UK. Where a candidate makes more evaluative points than are required to gain the maximum allocation of **4 marks**, these can be credited as knowledge and understanding marks provided they meet the criteria for this.	12	*Evaluate the effectiveness of either prison sentences or community based sentences in tackling crime.* Credit responses that make reference to: • the role of prison sentences in tackling crime • an evaluation of the success/shortcomings of prison sentences in tackling crime Credit responses that make reference to: • the role of community based sentences in tackling crime • an evaluation of the success/shortcomings of community based sentences in tackling crime *Candidates can be credited in a number of ways **up to a maximum of 12 marks.*** **Possible approaches to answering the question:** **Response 1** • Prison is an effective way of tackling crime because someone who is locked up in prison is not free to be on the street and attack people (**1 mark KU**). **Response 2** • Prison is not an effective way of tackling crime as prisons are often overcrowded and short-staffed. This means that prisoners are often locked up for most of the day and prisons are unable to carry out much rehabilitation — such as education classes to give prisoners skills to help them get a job when they are released from prison. As a result, there is a high rate of recidivism with people who are released from prison going on to commit more crimes and being returned to prison for another sentence (**2 marks KU, 1 mark evaluation**). **Response 3** • Prison can be an effective method of tackling crime as it involves the loss of freedom and so is a form of punishment. This will act as a deterrent to many people and stop them from committing a crime as they would fear being locked up for a period of time away from their friends and families (**2 marks evaluation**). **Response 4** • Community based sentences are very effective in tackling crime as they allow offenders to maintain daily contact with their family and loved ones. This means they do not feel isolated and do not grow anxious about the events affecting their family while they are in prison. If an offender is placed on a Community Order they will be ordered to carry out a certain number of hours of work which they can do in their spare time, allowing them to keep their job. This is an obvious advantage in stopping recidivism. Part of the order may also see them being given help for any addiction issues they may have. This sense of value that is created in the offender will make them much less likely to re-offend and the financial cost to the community will be low eg average cost of a Community Payback Order is only £2400 (**2 marks KU, 2 marks evaluation**). **Response 5** • The majority of the public think community based sentences are no more than a slap on the wrists for criminals. It is clear they have little impact on crime by the fact that around 30% on CPOs breach the orders and use the opportunity to further offend (**1 mark KU, 1 mark evaluation**). *Any other valid point that meets the criteria described in the general marking principles for this kind of question.*

Question	General Marking Instructions for this type of question	Max marks	Specific Marking Instructions for this question
4.	The candidate is required to interpret/evaluate up to three complex sources in order to reach conclusions. In order to achieve credit candidates must show evidence which explains the conclusions reached. Award up to **3 marks** for appropriate use of evidence depending on the quality of the explanation and the synthesis of the evidence to reach any one conclusion. For **full marks** candidates must refer to all sources in their answer. For **full marks** candidates must reach conclusions about each of the points given and make an overall conclusion on the issue.	8	*What conclusions can be drawn about the impact of the recession on different EU members?* *Candidates can be credited in a number of ways up to a maximum of 8 marks.* **Possible approaches to answering the question:** **The economic impact of the recession on Eurozone members** **Response 1** • Source A states that, the recession led to some serious long term economic problems for Eurozone countries. This is supported by Source B which shows that the biggest increase in unemployment was in Cyprus, where it quadrupled. This shows that the recession has had a huge impact on the Eurozone countries **(2 marks, synthesis of evidence across Sources A and B with conclusion).** **Response 2** • The recession clearly had a negative effect on all Eurozone countries but not all to the same extent. This is shown by the example of Spain from Source B which has a debt of 72% of its GDP which is lower than the EU average of 89% and by the example of Ireland which was more seriously affected as its debt has increased to 123% of GDP, which is much higher than the EU figure and is nearly five times higher than it was **(3 marks for complex synthesis between Sources A and B and a conclusion).** **The economic impact of the recession on Non-Eurozone members** **Response 3** • The recession had smaller effect on Non-Eurozone countries. As Source C shows Denmark has seen its unemployment rate rise to 7% but this is 3% less than the EU average **(2 marks, detailed synthesis across Sources A and C).** **Response 4** • The recession has not had such a serious effect on Non-Eurozone members. Several Eurozone countries have required "hand-outs" from the EU to help them cope with their huge debts eg both Ireland and Spain needed a 90billion Euro hand-out. This hasn't been needed for any non-Eurozone countries who all, apart from the UK, have a level of debt below the EU figure (89% of GDP). In fact, one non Eurozone country, Sweden, did not increase its levels of debt at all as a result of the recession. All of the Non-Eurozone countries in Source C have unemployment rates below the EU average **(3 marks synthesis and detailed use of sources).** **Possible overall conclusion about the impact of the recession on the EU as a whole** **Response 5** • The overall conclusion is that the EU as a whole has suffered badly from the recession but the Eurozone members suffered the most. Source A shows that the level of exports to countries outside the EU has dropped by 4% which may have resulted in the large increases in unemployment and debt levels in countries like Portugal **(2 marks for a valid overall conclusion based on evidence).** **Response 6** • The overall conclusion is that the recession has not had an equal impact across the EU's members. Some have suffered very badly from higher unemployment and debt eg Spain unemployment doubled and they need a bail out to survive whereas the UK had only a small increase in unemployment and Sweden did not increase its borrowing at all **(2 marks for a valid overall conclusion based on evidence).** Please note that a valid conclusion which is not supported with relevant source evidence should be given no credit. *Any other valid point that meets the criteria described in the general marking principles for this kind of question.*

Section 3 — International Issues

Question		General Marking Instructions for this type of question	Max marks	Specific Marking Instructions for this question
5.	(a)	An analysis mark should be awarded where a candidate uses their knowledge and understanding/a source to identify relevant components (eg of an idea, theory, argument, etc) and clearly show at least one of the following: • links between different components • links between component(s) and the whole • links between component(s) and related concepts • similarities and contradictions • consistency and inconsistency • different views/interpretations • possible consequences/implications • the relative importance of components • understanding of underlying order or structure Up to **8 marks** for KU (description, explanation and exemplification) and up to **4 marks** for analytical comments. Award up to **6 marks** per point. Where a candidate makes more analytical points than are required to gain the maximum allocation of **4 marks**, these can be credited as knowledge and understanding marks provided they meet the criteria for this.	12	*With reference to a world power you have studied, analyse the ability of this world power to influence other countries.* Credit responses that make reference to: • the world power's unilateral influence on its neighbours • the importance of the world power in wider international relations eg through organisations such as the UN or NATO • overall evaluative comment on the importance of the world power in influencing other countries • provide a clear, coherent line of argument **Possible approaches to answering the question:** **World Power: USA** **Credit reference to aspects of the following:** • member of the UN Security Council • examples of US involvement in Afghanistan (ISAF) • leading role in NATO — examples of US involvement in Libya as part of Operation Unified Protector • possible future role of US in Syria • mèmber of the G8 • largest economy in the world • role in Middle East • nuclear superpower • impact of emergence of China as superpower • economic, social and cultural impact on immediate neighbours such as Mexico and Canada and on North/central America as a whole including Cuba *Any other valid point that meets the criteria described in the general marking principles for this kind of question.* **World Power: China** **Credit reference to aspects of the following:** • leading role as a permanent member of the UN Security Council • participates in UN peace-keeping operations • relationship with and future role in negotiations with North Korea • impact of US/China diplomatic relations • investment in African countries and elsewhere • growing importance of China in world economy (2nd to the USA and expected to pass) • member of the G20 • part of the G8's Outreach Five (O5) • economic, social and cultural impact on immediate neighbours such as India and North Korea and on Asia as a whole *Any other valid point that meets the criteria described in the general marking principles for this kind of question.* **Possible approaches to answering the question:** **World Power: USA** **Response 1** • The USA's role as a world power is very important. It was one of the original countries that set up NATO in 1949 and still remains its most influential member. More recently the USA has played the lead role in NATO's mission to Afghanistan (ISAF) **(2 marks KU).**

Question	General Marking Instructions for this type of question	Max marks	Specific Marking Instructions for this question
5. (a)	(continued)		**Response 2** • The USA's role as a world power is very important. It was one of the original countries that set up NATO in 1949 and still remains its most influential member. More recently the USA has played the lead role in NATO's mission to Afghanistan (ISAF). In terms of finance, troop and resource commitments to NATO, the USA provides far more than any other single member of the Alliance making the US the most important member of NATO with huge influence **(2 marks KU, 1 mark analysis)**. **Response 3** • The USA's role as a world power is very important. It was one of the original countries that set up NATO in 1949 and remains its most influential member. More recently the USA has played the lead role in NATO's mission to Afghanistan (ISAF). In terms of finance, troop and resource commitments to NATO, the USA provides far more than any other single member of the Alliance making the US the most important member of NATO with huge influence. However, in recent years the USA has called on the other members of NATO to pay a greater share of the organisation's costs. The USA has also reduced its commitments in Europe, expecting the European members of NATO to take over. Although the USA can dominate NATO in terms of its contribution, all NATO's 28 member states have equal standing, ie no one member country has more voting rights than the next and there must be agreement by all before action can be taken. The USA has huge influence, but NATO is not always obliged to follow its lead as the other members can out vote them. However, this does not always stop the USA which has the capacity to act alone **(2 marks KU, 4 marks analysis)**. **Response 4** • Therefore, given the importance of the USA within NATO, the UN, other international bodies and the global economy, it is clear the USA is, at present, the world's most influential country. For example, the US is sometimes described as 'the leader of the free world'. However, countries such as China and India are closing the gap in terms of economic output and world influence. Further, China has entered the space race and is increasing its influence in Africa. Also, despite US/NATO military strength in Afghanistan, they have failed to completely defeat the Taliban. The USA may be the worlds' only 'superpower' but this does not mean it can control everything **(4 marks analysis)**.

Question	General Marking Instructions for this type of question	Max marks	Specific Marking Instructions for this question

5. (b)	An analysis mark should be awarded where a candidate uses their knowledge and understanding/a source to identify relevant components (eg of an idea, theory, argument, etc) and clearly show at least one of the following:
	• links between different components
	• links between component(s) and the whole
	• links between component(s) and related concepts
	• similarities and contradictions
	• consistency and inconsistency
	• different views/interpretations
	• possible consequences/implications
	• the relative importance of components
	• understanding of underlying order or structure
	
	Up to **8 marks** for KU (description, explanation and exemplification) and up to **4 marks** for analytical comments.
	
	Award up to **6 marks** per point.
	
	Where a candidate makes more analytical points than are required to gain the maximum allocation of **4 marks**, these can be credited as knowledge and understanding marks provided they meet the criteria for this.
		12	*With reference to a world power you have studied, analyse the impact of a recent social issue on this world power.*
			Credit references that make reference to:
			• Description/explanation of the social issue
			• Impact of the social issue on specific groups or the country as a whole
			
			Candidates can be credited in a number of ways up to a maximum of 12 marks.
			Credit reference to aspects of the following:
			• Impact of issues concerning:
			  • Healthcare
			  • Education
			  • Housing
			  • Crime
			  • Population/Immigration
			  • Economy — welfare/poverty
			  • Environmental
			
			World Power Choice: India
			
			Response 1
			• The population of India has continued to grow in recent years. They now have 17% of the world's population (1.21 billion people). India is expected to have more people than China by the year 2030, creating huge problems for housing, healthcare etc **(2 marks KU).**
			
			Response 2
			• The population of India has continued to grow in recent years. They now have 17% of the world's population (1.21 billion people). India is expected to have more people than China by the year 2030, creating huge problems for housing, healthcare etc. The population has grown by 181 million in the last ten years putting massive pressure on already stretched educational services. On top of an extremely high birth rate life expectancy has grown by ten years to an average of 75. The demand for healthcare created by an ageing population is financially difficult for the government **(2 marks KU, 2 marks analysis).**
			
			Response 3
			• The population of India has continued to grow in recent years. They now have 17% of the world's population (1.21 billion people). India is expected to have more people than China by the year 2030, creating huge problems for housing, healthcare etc. The population has grown by 181 million in the last ten years putting massive pressure on already stretched educational services. On top of an extremely high birth rate life expectancy has grown by ten years to an average of 75. The demand for healthcare created by an ageing population is financially difficult for the government. The ageing of the population is perhaps the most serious social problem facing India. Over 100 million people are elderly and although over 60% of the population is under thirty the cost of healthcare and pensions for the elderly is enormous. The average Indian worker does not earn enough to pay large amounts of tax **(3 marks KU, 3 marks analysis).**
			
			Also credit reference to aspects of the following:
			• Growing economy
			• Widening gap between urban and rural areas
			• Women's rights and progress

Question	General Marking Instructions for this type of question	Max marks	Specific Marking Instructions for this question
5. (b)	(continued)		**World Power choice: China** **Response 4** • Rapid growth in the Chinese population has been a problem for many decades. Since the 1970s the Chinese Government has enforced measures to control the number of children people can have. Couples can have only one child in urban areas but can have two in rural areas, provided the first-born is a girl. This was known as the One Child Policy **(2 marks KU)**. **Response 5** • Rapid growth in the Chinese population has been a problem for many decades. Since the 1970s the Chinese Government has enforced measures to control the number of children people can have. Couples can have only one child in urban areas but can have two in rural areas, provided the first-born is a girl. This was known as the One Child Policy. Punishments for couples who had too many children ranged from fines, loss of employment to forced abortions and sterilizations during the later stages of their pregnancy **(3 marks KU)**. **Response 6** • Rapid growth in the Chinese population has been a problem for many decades. Since the 1970s the Chinese Government has enforced measures to control the number of children people can have. Couples can have only one child in urban areas but can have two in rural areas, provided the first-born is a girl. This was known as the One Child Policy. Punishments for couple who had too many children ranged from fines, loss of employment to forced abortions and sterilizations during the later stages of their pregnancy. The policy was strictly enforced throughout the final decades of the twentieth century and as a result there has been an increase in the number of children forced to carry the burden of caring for ageing parents on their own. Fewer girls than boys survived to adulthood as many people, especially in rural areas, abandoned or killed their first born baby if it was a girl. In many traditional areas boys became even more valuable than girls. This created a gender imbalance affecting the population and the economy. However there is evidence that the One Child Policy will be relaxed in some areas. Families will be allowed two children if one parent is an only child and fines have been lowered **(4 marks KU, 3 marks analysis)**. **Also credit reference to aspects of the following:** • Widening gap between rural and urban areas • Impact of growing economy and investment in market economy • Media censorship

Question		General Marking Instructions for this type of question	Max marks	Specific Marking Instructions for this question
5.	(c)	An analysis mark should be awarded where a candidate uses their knowledge and understanding/a source to identify relevant components (eg of an idea, theory, argument, etc) and clearly show at least one of the following: • links between different components • links between component(s) and the whole • links between component(s) and related concepts • similarities and contradictions • consistency and inconsistency • different views/interpretations • possible consequences/implications • the relative importance of components • understanding of underlying order or structure Up to **8 marks** for KU (description, explanation and exemplification) and up to **4 marks** for analytical comments Award up to **6 marks** per point. Where a candidate makes more analytical points than are required to gain the maximum allocation of **4 marks**, these can be credited as knowledge and understanding marks provided they meet the criteria for this.	12	*With reference to a world issue you have studied, analyse the role of international organisations in attempting to resolve this issue* *Candidates can be credited in a number of ways up to a maximum of 12 marks.* Depending on the world issue chosen, candidates may analyse aspects such as: • The nature of issue • The international organisations involved • The nature of responses to the organisation's actions • Success and failure of the organisation's actions and the reasons for these successes and failures **Poverty in Africa:** **Response 1** • Poverty in Africa is often caused by ill-health. One of the most serious diseases in Africa is Malaria which affects millions of Africans, killing hundreds of thousands every year. People who are ill cannot work and so they and their families fall deeper into poverty. The World Health Organisation (WHO), which is part of the United Nations, is responsible for improving health around the world. The WHO has attempted to tackle malaria by providing drugs to treat people in poor areas. They have also provided millions of nets sprayed with insecticide to protect people when they are sleeping or praying. This is an effective way of controlling the mosquitoes which spread the disease and has resulted in many saved lives. However, their response to malaria is still considered inadequate by many as each of these nets only costs a few pounds yet one African child dies every sixty seconds as a result of malaria **(3 marks KU, 2 marks analysis)**. **Response 2** • During recent civil wars many people have become refugees as their homes have been destroyed by armed men. They now live in poverty as a result **(1 mark KU)**. **Response 3** • Many children in countries like Botswana have been left orphaned by AIDS. This has denied them an education and resulted in a lifetime of poverty. Their health will also be affected as what little healthcare that may be available, they will be unable to afford **(2 marks KU)**. **Syria:** • condemnation of Syrian government by UN, Arab League, western countries • sanctions, including economic sanctions • UN investigation/inspection of use of chemical weapons • humanitarian assistance for refugees • aid to anti-government forces • threats of military action/intervention **Terrorism:** • Growth of IS, Boko Haram, Al-Shabaab etc • "home-grown" terrorists — Paris attacks etc • Religious/ethnic/political conflicts • NATO — Article 5 (Collective defence), vast resources committed by NATO, Operation Active Endeavour, help in providing security at major events such as Olympic games and European Football championships etc.

Question		General Marking Instructions for this type of question	Max marks	Specific Marking Instructions for this question
5.	(c)	(continued)		• The UN — coordinating action through the Security Council and the General Assembly, The United Nations Global Counter-Terrorism Strategy • The African Union Counter Terrorism framework • The European Union Counter terrorism Strategy — focusing on stopping the causes of radicalisation and recruitment etc, tries to improve the sharing of information between member states, European arrest warrant strengthened etc *Any other valid point that meets the criteria described in the general marking principles for this kind of question.*

5.	(d)	An analysis mark should be awarded where a candidate uses their knowledge and understanding/a source to identify relevant components (eg of an idea, theory, argument, etc) and clearly show at least one of the following:
		• links between different components
		• links between component(s) and the whole
		• links between component(s) and related concepts
		• similarities and contradictions
		• consistency and inconsistency
		• different views/interpretations
		• possible consequences/implications
		• the relative importance of components
		• understanding of underlying order or structure
		
		Up to **8 marks** for KU (description, explanation and exemplification) and up to **4 marks** for analytical comments.
		
		Award up to **6 marks** per point.
		
		Where a candidate makes more analytical points than are required to gain the maximum allocation of **4 marks**, these can be credited as knowledge and understanding marks provided they meet the criteria for this.
			12	*With reference to a world issue you have studied; analyse the different factors which have caused this issue.*
				
				*Candidates can be credited in a number of ways **up to a maximum of 12 marks**.*
				
				Depending on the world issue chosen candidates may make reference to any relevant factors, such as:
				• political factors
				• economic factors
				• social factors
				Low level of economic development:
				
				Response 1
				Illness and the lack of appropriate medical facilities contribute to the low level of economic development in many parts of Africa. For example, over half a million people die in sub-Saharan Africa each year because of malaria. Malaria reduces the ability to work and save so families cannot meet their needs. In this situation it is difficult for countries to develop their own industries and infrastructure. As a result foreign companies are unwilling to invest or commit their employees to the country. If African governments could provide anti-malaria facilities and equipment then educational attainment would improve and the economy would grow. Such developments however, will take many years to succeed and governments may require foreign aid to do this **(2 marks KU, 2 marks analysis)**.
				
				Arab spring:
				• dissatisfaction with the role of government in a range of countries, including:
				  • protests against dictatorships
				  • lack of human rights
				  • corruption
				• economic issues, including:
				  • economic decline
				  • unemployment
				  • food price rises
				  • extreme poverty
				• social factors, including:
				  • large numbers of disenchanted but highly educated young people
				  • use of social media to inform and spread protests
				
				Any other valid point that meets the criteria described in the general marking principles for this kind of question.

HIGHER MODERN STUDIES
2016

Section 1 — Democracy in Scotland and the United Kingdom

Question	General Marking Instructions for this type of question	Max marks	Specific Marking Instructions for this question
1.	The candidate is required to interpret/ evaluate up to three complex sources in order to reach conclusions. In order to achieve credit candidates must show evidence which explains the conclusions reached. Award up to **3 marks** for appropriate use of evidence depending on the quality of the explanation and the synthesis of the evidence to reach any one conclusion. For **full marks** candidates must refer to all sources in their answer. For **full marks** candidates must reach conclusions about each of the points given and make an overall conclusion on the issue.	8	*Candidates can be credited in a number of ways up to a maximum of 8 marks.* **Possible approaches to answering the question:** **The link between government policy and the turnout of different age groups** **Response 1** The turnout of different age groups depends on which group is targeted by the government. Younger voters are less likely to vote (only 43% for youngest group). This has been caused by the government aiming policies at older groups who are much more likely to vote, e.g. 65s and over *(2 marks for synthesis of evidence across Sources A and B with conclusion).* **Response 2** Specific policies like the abolition of the EMA have led to lower turnout by young voters. This stands at 35% less than the oldest age group. This policy may not affect older people directly, whereas the increase in the flat rate pension will benefit many of them greatly. As older people are more likely to vote, government policies are more likely to benefit them which in turn leads to even higher turnouts among the over 65s *(3 marks for synthesis between Sources A, B and C and a conclusion).* **Response 3** Different government policies lead to different turnout rates in different age groups *(0 marks for conclusion with no supporting evidence).* **The link between government policy and the turnout of different socio-economic groups** **Response 4** Different government policies lead to different turnout rates in different socio-economic groups. The wealthiest groups like social classes A and B are most likely to vote *(1 mark for conclusion and correct use of Source A).* **Response 5** Government policies aimed at certain socio-economic groups have a huge effect on the turnout at elections of these groups. For example, those who rent their house either privately or socially are the least likely groups to vote. Those who own their own homes are not affected by government policies like the bedroom tax which will see some benefits removed from those who rent. This means that they will be more likely to vote, as is proven in Source B where home owners have the highest turnout at 77%. As these wealthier groups are more likely to vote then governments will continue to "pass laws which benefit the groups most likely to vote" Source A *(3 marks for conclusion backed by detailed use of sources and synthesis).* **Possible overall conclusion about turnout in the UK** **Response 6** The overall conclusion is that turnout in the UK is increasing *(0 marks for overall conclusion without supporting evidence).*

Question		General Marking Instructions for this type of question	Max marks	Specific Marking Instructions for this question
1.		(continued)		**Response 7** The overall conclusion is that turnout in the UK is increasing. Source B tells me it went from 65.1% in 2010 to 66.1% in 2015 *(1 mark for a valid overall conclusion based on evidence)*. **Response 8** The overall conclusion is that turnout in the UK is increasing. Source B tells me it has steadily increased from 59.4% in 2001 to 66.1% in 2015. There was only a small 1% increase in 2015 largely caused by the massive jump in turnout in Scotland caused by the referendum *(2 marks for a valid overall conclusion based on evidence from two sources)*. **Response 9** Overall, turnout level in UK elections is very uneven between different ages and groups. Older people (65+) are almost twice as likely to vote than younger groups (18–24). Those in more affluent group such as home owners and class A/B are also more likely to vote *(2 marks for a valid overall conclusion based on evidence from two sources)*. **Please note that a valid conclusion which is not supported with relevant source evidence should be given no credit.** *Any other valid point that meets the criteria described in the general marking principles for this kind of question.*
2.	(a)	An analysis mark should be awarded where a candidate uses their knowledge and understanding/a source, to identify relevant components (e.g. of an idea, theory, argument, etc.) and clearly show at least one of the following: • links between different components • links between component(s) and the whole • links between components(s) and related concepts • similarities and contradictions • consistency and inconsistency • different views/interpretations • possible consequences/implications • the relative importance of components • understanding of underling order or structure Up to **8 marks** for KU (description, explanation and exemplification) and up to **4 marks** for analytical comments. Award up to **6 marks** per point Candidates should be credited up to **full marks** if they answer within a Scottish context only, a UK context only or refer to both Scotland and the UK as appropriate. Where a candidate makes more evaluative points than are required to gain the maximum allocation of **4 marks**, these can be credited as knowledge and understanding marks provided they meet the criteria for this.	12	*Candidates can be credited in a number of ways up to a maximum of 12 marks.* **Credit reference to aspects of the following:** *Additional Member System:* • Two votes so more opportunity to choose candidates from a minority group, better representing their views. • The degree of proportionality allows for a wider range of parties to gain representation providing better representation. • Constituency and list representatives gives more choice of representative for voters. • Parties are more easily held to account. • Likelihood of coalition (not recently) forces a wider range of views to be considered. *Balanced by:* • Recent elections show that majority governments can be elected on a minority of the vote due to the FPTP element of AMS. • Coalitions are perhaps not representative as this "compromise" did not appear on the ballot paper. • Two ballot papers could be confusing, increasing voter apathy, lowering turnouts and therefore leading to the underrepresentation of sections of society. • Link between constituency and representative is weakened. *First Past the Post:* • Link between representative and constituency is clear and improves representation of views due to direct accountability. • Usually produces a majority, single party government which can legislate in line with promises without compromise.

Question		General Marking Instructions for this type of question	Max marks	Specific Marking Instructions for this question
2.	(a)	(continued)		**Balanced by:** • In UK elections it has favoured two large parties for many years. In Scotland it exaggerated the representation of the Labour Party for many decades. • Views not well represented due to the creation of many safe seats. • Lack of proportionality between number of votes and number of seats, e.g. 2015 election. • Tactical voting is possible and is often actively encouraged. This means the views of the electorate are not well represented as many vote for candidates they don't actually agree with. **Single Transferable Vote:** • Voters can choose between candidates from within the same party, improving the representation of their views. • The degree of proportionality allows for a wider range of parties to gain representation providing better representation. • Multi-member wards allow voters to select candidates from different parties. • Greater likelihood of coalition in councils forces a wider range of views to be considered. **Balanced by:** • Coalitions are perhaps not representative as this "compromise" did not appear on the ballot paper. • Link between constituency and representative is weakened. **Regional Lists:** • Provides a high degree of proportionality, reflecting voters' views. • Large regions allow parties with "thinly-spread" support to gain representation. **Balanced by:** • Too much power is given to parties to select candidates on the list. • Link between constituency and representative is weakened. *Any other valid point that meets the criteria described in the general marking principles for this type of question.* **Possible approaches to answering the question:** **Response 1** The Scottish Parliament uses the Additional Member System (AMS) to elect 129 MSPs split between 73 constituencies and 8 regional lists *(1 mark KU)*. AMS allows each voter two separate votes, one for their constituency MSP and one for their region, providing better representation for their views *(1 mark analysis)*. (Total 2 marks — 1 mark KU, 1 mark analysis) **Response 2** The Scottish Parliament uses the Additional Member System (AMS) to elect 129 MSPs split between 73 constituencies and 8 regional lists *(1 mark KU)*. Voters have one vote for a constituency MSP and one vote for a regional list MSP which could lead to a higher turnout if voters know their second vote helps elect a regional MSP from the party they support *(1 mark KU, 1 mark analysis)*. The constituency FPTP element of AMS, only allows voters to have one choice for a constituency MSP. This has led to the claim that many votes are "wasted" because with FPTP, only votes for the winning candidate matter. Second-placed candidates get nothing *(1 mark analysis)*. (Total 4 marks — 2 marks KU, 2 marks analysis)

Question		General Marking Instructions for this type of question	Max marks	Specific Marking Instructions for this question
2.	(a)	(continued)		**Response 3** Systems of proportional representation such as the Additional Member System are said to be fairer and provide for better representation of the views of the electorate. Since devolution, Scotland has used AMS to elect the 129 MSPs, a mixture of FPTP to elect constituency MSPs and regional list to elect "top up" MSPs *(1 mark KU)*. Tactical voting is still possible in the First Past the Post constituency ballot, which affects the accuracy of the result but this is balanced by the second ballot which uses a regional list system, creating a more proportional result *(1 mark KU, 1 mark analysis)*. Each voter has a total of 8 MSPs to represent their views. This extra choice allows for more participation and a much higher level of representation. Voters can contact the MSP who best represents their political views *(1 mark KU, 1 mark analysis)*. **(Total 5 marks — 3 marks KU, 2 marks analysis)** **Response 4** First Past the Post is used across the UK to elect 650 MPs to the Westminster Parliament. Each voter selects the candidate they want and whichever one gets the most votes wins the constituency and a seat in parliament. The winner does not need more than 50% of the total vote. In some marginal constituencies the winning candidate may only receive around 30% of the total vote. **(Total — 2 marks KU)** **Response 5** The single transferable vote (STV) system improves the representation of the electorate's views as there is a close relationship between the proportion of votes gained by a party and the number of councillors they win. A PR system like this allows those voters who support smaller parties like the Greens, to confidently vote for them knowing that a simple majority is not required, as it is in the traditionally used First Past the Post system. This proportionality is the main strength of STV and allows the views of voters to be extremely well represented. **(Total 4 marks — 2 marks KU, 2 marks analysis)** *Any other valid point that meets the criteria described in the general marking instructions for this kind of question.*
2.	(b)	An analysis mark should be awarded where a candidate uses their knowledge and understanding/a source, to identify relevant components (e.g. of an idea, theory, argument, etc.) and clearly show at least one of the following: • links between different components • links between component(s) and the whole • links between components(s) and related concepts • similarities and contradictions • consistency and inconsistency • different views/interpretations • possible consequences/implications • the relative importance of components • understanding of underling order or structure Up to **8 marks** for KU (description, explanation and exemplification) and up to **4 marks** for analytical comments.	12	*Candidates can be credited in a number of ways **up to a maximum of 12 marks.*** **Credit reference to aspects of the following:** • Ways in which groups in society seek to influence decision making in government • Use of campaigns by groups and organisations designed to impact upon decision making in government, e.g. media campaigns, petitions, lobbying, rallies/demonstrations, etc. • Increase of direct action campaigns — Occupy Movement, Anonymous Organisation, the 99%, Student Protests in England and Wales, Anti-Fracking campaigns, Third Runway and HS2 Opposition • Individual backing of Campaigns by MPs, e.g. Greg Mulholland MP and the Aims of the Campaign for Real Ale (removal of beer duty escalator) Tom Watson MP and anti-hacking campaign • Evidence of very close links between commercial organisations and government, e.g. News International and various governments, Levenson Inquiry and links between PM and senior News Int. execs.

Question	General Marking Instructions for this type of question	Max marks	Specific Marking Instructions for this question
2. (b)	(continued) Award up to **6 marks** per point. Candidates should be credited up to **full marks** if they answer within a Scottish context only, a UK context only or refer to both Scotland and the UK as appropriate. Where a candidate makes more evaluative points than are required to gain the maximum allocation of **4 marks**, these can be credited as knowledge and understanding marks provided they meet the criteria for this.		• Differences between the effect of some groups in influencing decision making than others, e.g. Insider groups/outsider groups. Sectional interest groups exist to promote interests of their members (Trade Unions/CBI). Single Issue groups to promote a particular issue or viewpoint (Stop the War Campaign, Axe the Bedroom Tax) • Voting — more influential in some circumstances, e.g. marginal constituencies • Individual contacting representatives, e.g. surgeries • Influence of the Civil Service on Governmental Decision making • Use of e-petitions to shape Governmental business and discussion • The ways in which some pressure groups use the media to influence decision making through public opinion and their effectiveness • Backing of MPs by trade unions and private businesses. Limit and extent of influence of Trade Unions and private businesses • Use of social media and internet including Twitter, Facebook, Youtube by groups and individuals to galvanise public opinion and influence governmental decision making • Concern of extent and influence of paid lobbyists within House of Lords and the Commons • Proposals for statutory register of lobbyists to identify who they act on behalf of as well as a limit on expenditure by organisations and lobbyists (but excluding Political Parties) during the general election. Concern by charities and academics that the Lobbying Bill could undermine "fabric of democracy" • Allegations of paid relationships between lobbyists and members of House of Lords. Suspension of members of HofL due to closeness to lobbyists and conflict of interest • Ability of MPs, HofLs, Parliamentary Committees in influencing in Government decision making *Any other valid point that meets the criteria described in the general marking instructions for this kind of question.* **Possible approaches to answering this question:** **Response 1** Some commentators and politicians believe that the links between some MPs, Members of the House of Lords and some paid lobbyists are far too close and may harm the democratic process. Some MPs and Lords are paid as consultants for companies and many see this as a conflict of interest between their constituents and the companies that pay them *(1 mark KU, 1 mark analysis)*. **Response 2** The Labour Party is concerned about the number of hedge funds and City of London firms who donate regularly to the Conservative Party and, in return, the Conservatives complain about the link between individual Labour MPs, the Labour Party and the Trade Union movement *(1 mark KU)*. This has led government to introduce proposals for a statutory register of lobbyists and a limit on the amount that organisations can spend during a General Election. Some charities and academics have said that these proposals could undermine the "fabric of democracy". This not just shows that some people are concerned about the effects that lobbyists have on decision making but also that new proposals to limit group's abilities to affect change in government could actually limit decision making and democracy *(2 marks analysis)*. **(Total 5 marks — 2 marks KU, 3 marks analysis)**

Question		General Marking Instructions for this type of question	Max marks	Specific Marking Instructions for this question
2.	(b)	(continued)		**Response 3** Some groups outside of Parliament are more effective than others in influencing Governmental decision making. For example, insider groups can be said to be more successful and effective in influencing government policy than outsider groups. An insider group generally have strong links to the government and are usually regularly asked by the government for their opinion and ideas on areas that they are familiar with. *(1 mark KU, 1 mark analysis)*. Insider groups usually represent a specific interest or section of society, e.g. The British Medical Association (BMA) or Confederation of British Industry. Trade Unions can also be seen as an insider group, for example, the teacher's Union in Scotland, the EIS, is regularly consulted by the Scottish Government over education issues such as the introduction of the Curriculum for Excellence *(2 marks KU)*. (Total 4 marks — 3 marks KU, 1 mark analysis) **Response 4** Government may involve insider groups in decision making as they tend to be very knowledgeable about their specific area of interest and as a consequence, government will use their expertise when drafting policies or laws *(1 mark analysis)*. For example, Government sought the advice of the CBI over the proposed increase in the National Minimum Wage as well as when the government were creating new legislation limiting the number of non EU workers doing various types of work in the UK *(2 marks KU)*. However, outsider groups often struggle to make government listen or influence the decisions they make. It may be because the group's demands are not in line with the government's policies. For example, The Stop the War coalition against war in Iraq and Afghanistan demonstrated in London with over a million demonstrators protesting. Despite it being the largest demonstration ever in the UK, the government still went ahead and sent British soldiers to war. Therefore, this shows that some groups are more successful than others with insider groups often being more influential than outsider groups *(1 mark KU, 2 marks analysis)*. (Total 6 marks — 3 marks KU, 3 marks analysis)

Section 2 – Social Issues in the United Kingdom

Part A: Social inequality in the United Kingdom

Question	General Marking Instructions for this type of question	Max marks	Specific Marking Instructions for this question
3. (a)	An analysis mark should be awarded where a candidate uses their knowledge and understanding/a source, to identify relevant components (e.g. of an idea, theory, argument, etc.) and clearly show at least one of the following: • links between different components • links between component(s) and the whole • links between components(s) and related concepts • similarities and contradictions • consistency and inconsistency • different views/interpretations • possible consequences/implications • the relative importance of components • understanding of underling order or structure Evaluation involves making a judgments based on criteria, drawing conclusions on the extent to which a view is supported by the evidence; counter-arguments including possible alternative interpretations; the overall impact/significance of the factors when taken together; the relative importance of factors in relation to the context. Credit responses that make reference to: • Government policies • Analysis/evaluation of the impact that these policies have had on reducing inequalities • Balanced overall evaluative comment on the effectiveness of government policies in reducing inequalities • Provide a clear, coherent line of argument **General Marking Instructions** Candidates should be credited up to full marks if they answer within a Scottish context only, a UK context only or refer to both Scotland and the UK as appropriate. Up to **8 marks** for KU (description, explanation and exemplification) and up to **12 marks** for analytical/ evaluative comments. Award up to **6 marks** per point. Where a candidate makes more analytical/evaluative points than are required to gain the maximum allocation of 8 marks, these can be credited as knowledge and understanding marks provided they meet the criteria for this.	20	Government policies have failed to reduce social inequalities. Discuss. *Candidates can be credited in a number of ways up to a maximum of 20 marks.* **Credit reference to aspects of the following:** • Recent government policies • Analysis/evaluation of the impact that these policies have had on reducing inequalities • Balanced overall evaluative comment on the effectiveness of government policies in reducing inequalities • Provide a clear, coherent line of argument Wide range of Welfare State provision including State benefits, healthcare, education, housing and personal/ children's social services, employment services. • Debate over access, quality and extent of State support including introduction of means-testing of Child Benefit, tightening of benefit rules, etc. The removal of some universal benefits. Under-26s unable to claim housing benefit. • Equalities legislation including Equality Act 2012 as well as The Commission for Equality and Human Rights; Gender Equality Duty Code of Practice; Women's Enterprise Task Force. • The introduction of the Universal Credit, cap on benefit limits, "bedroom tax", etc. • Credit candidates who make reference to/comment on Scottish government policies, e.g. end of prescription charges, free personal care for the elderly, etc. • Previous government policies – Tax Credits system, National Minimum Wage, work of equal value, changes in maternity and paternity leave arrangements. • Reference to official reports, e.g. poverty levels among pensioners and children, unemployment statistics, statistics on inequalities by socioeconomic group, gender, race, etc. Stats may cover income, wealth, education and health outcomes, etc. • Poverty reduction targets (children, fuel poverty) not being met but some progress being made, e.g. just under 20% of children (2.3m) lived in households classed as below poverty line in 2012 a drop of 2% or 300,000 children from year before. Numbers in severe poverty also fell. Child poverty groups claim figure is higher, nearer 4m or more than 1 in 4 of all children. CPAG claims figure will rise in future as cap on benefits and bedroom tax begin to hit the poorest sections of society. • The poorest 10% of population have, on average, seen a fall in their real incomes after deducting housing costs, changes in benefits, etc. The richest 10% have seen bigger proportional rises in their income than any other group. There is growing evidence of inequality between the very rich and the very poor within UK. The UK's Gini Co-efficient is rising and higher than any point in last thirty years. OECD claims inequality rising faster in UK than any other rich nation. • Gender pay gap: UK women in full time work earn 10% less per hour (2012). Gender pay gap is bigger for part time work. Four in five paid carers are women. The care sector's poor pay contributes greatly to the gender pay gap. However, pay gap narrowing in some areas of employment.

Question	General Marking Instructions for this type of question	Max marks	Specific Marking Instructions for this question
3. (a)	(continued)		• Women make up 60% of the university population; success of women in reaching senior posts varies from place to place. "Glass ceiling" only cracked, not broken. • Women make up 29% of MPs (Increased from 22% in 2010); 19% of directors in FTSE 100 firms are women (increased from 12% in 2010) despite accounting for over 46% of the labour force. • Unemployment is higher amongst minority groups; far higher for 18–24 year olds; employment rates for ethnic minority groups lower but gap narrowing. • There is growing evidence of a "race pay gap". Women from Black Caribbean, Pakistani and Bangladeshi groups most likely to face a higher risk of unemployment, lower pay and have fewer prospects for promotion. • Any other valid point. *Any other valid point that meets the criteria described in the general marking instructions for this kind of question.* **Possible approaches to answering this question:** **Response 1** Governments have introduced various laws and policies to help to try and tackle some inequalities in the UK. These laws and policies include the Equality Act 2010, Working Tax Credits or the National Minimum Wage *(1 mark KU)*. **Response 2** Some people argue that changes in the benefits system made by the Coalition government led to growing inequalities and increased poverty for some sections of society particularly the low paid and those receiving benefits *(1 mark analysis)*. The Coalition Govt. cut the benefits budget as part of their austerity programme following the world recession. This has led to many of the poorest people in the UK being worse off as some benefits were scrapped and new changes introduced. The creation of Universal Credit, the "Bedroom tax" and limits on the amount of benefits that people receive has created further hardship for some families and may have may even have increased child poverty *(1 mark KU, 1 mark analysis, 1 mark evaluative comment)*. However, government policies have also indirectly benefited some groups. The National Minimum wage has benefited 2 million workers with 75% of these being women and ethnic minorities. However, many feel that the levels of the minimum wage are too low and are campaigning for a Living Wage increase to this policy. This shows that the policy has benefited people but that it also doesn't go far enough to fully tackle some inequalities *(1 mark KU, 1 mark evaluative comment)*. **(Total 7 marks – 2 marks KU, 2 marks analysis, 2 marks evaluative comment)** **Response 3** Despite legislation such as the 2010 Equality Act making it illegal for employers to discriminate against someone on the basis of gender, race, religion, sexuality, etc., discrimination still takes place. For example, 30,000 women every year are forced to leave their job every year due to pregnancy *(1 mark KU, 1 mark analysis)*. This shows that even with laws in place, discrimination does still happen. Men may earn around 18% more than women but the gap between male and female earnings is getting smaller and this demonstrates that the "pay gap" between men and women is improving but there is a long way to go before women and men achieve pay equality *(1 mark KU, 1 mark evaluative comment)*. **(Total 4 marks – 2 marks KU, 1 mark analysis, 1 mark evaluation)**

Question		General Marking Instructions for this type of question	Max marks	Specific Marking Instructions for this question
3.	(a)	(continued)		**Response 4** Despite the introduction of the Equality Act, discrimination still exists but many women are now obtaining high status jobs in companies and organisations, for example, over 60% of HR directors in the City of London are female but only occupy 30% of managing director positions. **(Total 2 marks – 1 mark KU, 1 mark evaluation)**
3.	(b)	An analysis mark should be awarded where a candidate uses their knowledge and understanding/a source, to identify relevant components (e.g. of an idea, theory, argument, etc.) and clearly show at least one of the following: • links between different components • links between component(s) and the whole • links between components(s) and related concepts • similarities and contradictions • consistency and inconsistency • different views/interpretations • possible consequences/implications • the relative importance of components • understanding of underling order or structure Evaluation involves making judgements based on criteria, drawing conclusions on the extent to which a view is supported by the evidence; counter-arguments including possible alternative interpretations; the overall impact/significance of the factors when taken together; the relative importance of factors in relation to the context. Credit responses that make reference to: • Theories of the causes of crime • Analysis of the importance of human nature as the main cause of crime • Balanced overall evaluative comment on the importance of human nature as the main cause of crime • Provide a clear, coherent line of argument Up to **8 marks** for KU (description, explanation and exemplification) and up to **12 marks** for analytical/evaluative comments. Award up to **6 marks** per point. Candidates should be credited up to **full marks** if they answer within a Scottish context only, a UK context only or refer to both Scotland and the UK as appropriate. Where a candidate makes more analytical/evaluative points than are required to gain the maximum allocation of **4 marks**, these can be credited as knowledge and understanding marks provided they meet the criteria for this.	20	*Candidates can be credited in a number of ways **up to a maximum of 20 marks.*** **Credit reference to aspects of the following:** • Poor lifestyle choices include smoking, excess alcohol consumption, lack of exercise, a diet high in salt and fat, drug misuse, or other risk-taking activities • Failure to make best use of preventative care services • Reference to government policies or health initiatives where it is acknowledged that these are a response to poor lifestyle choices, e.g. minimum alcohol pricing • Reference to official reports, e.g. Equally Well 2008 (and Inequalities Task Force Report 2010) • Statistical examples that highlight poor health in Scotland and/or the UK, e.g. the big five *Any other valid point that meets the criteria described in the general marking principles for this kind of question.* **Possible approaches to answering the question:** **Response 1** Some people choose to drink too much alcohol. Scotland has a culture of binge drinking especially at the weekend which costs the country a great deal of money *(1 mark KU).* **Response 2** Poor diet is a problem in Scottish society. Many people choose to eat too much fatty food such as burgers and chips. Health campaigns such as the 5-a-day campaign to encourage people to eat more fruit and vegetables are a response to too many people choosing to eat a poor diet *(2 marks KU).* **Response 3** Despite years of anti-smoking health campaigns or the ban on smoking in public places, some individuals continue to choose to smoke cigarettes. Around 22% of adults smoked in Scotland in 2012 *(1 mark KU, 1 mark analysis).* As a consequence of smoking an individual is more likely to suffer from respiratory illness or lung cancer. Around 90% of all lung cancer deaths are linked to people who smoked before they died. Therefore it is clear that lifestyle choices have a massive impact on health *(1 mark KU, 1 mark evaluation).* **(Total 4 marks – 2 marks KU, 1 mark analysis, 1 mark evaluation)** **Response 4** There are many lifestyle choices that can be made to improve health. People can choose not to smoke, drink too much alcohol or eat too much fatty food *(1 mark KU).* Statistics show that Scotland has many people who make the wrong lifestyle choices, e.g. around one in five adults smoke *(1 mark KU).* Choosing to take regular exercise is another important way that people can stay fit and healthy. Walking or cycling to school or work regularly has been proven to improve people's health. Many people in Scotland don't take regular exercise.

Question	General Marking Instructions for this type of question	Max marks	Specific Marking Instructions for this question
3. (b)	(continued)		Studies show that less than half the adult population takes an hour's exercise at least three times per week *(2 marks KU)*. In Scotland the government has tried to tackle ill-health by encouraging people to take more exercise however the people that have taken up the opportunities are more often the affluent rather than the poorest. Despite the Equally Well Report of 2008 recognising that there was a need to promote exercise there is still a clear need for Scotland to make better lifestyle choices to improve health *(2 marks analysis)*.
			(Total 6 marks — 4 marks KU, 2 marks analysis)
			Response 5 Overall, it is clear that lifestyle choices have a huge impact on an individual's health. However, what is also clear is that an individual's economic position will influence these choices. A healthy diet or a gym membership, are both more affordable for the middle classes who are more likely to have a comfortable income. Not all middle class people will make the healthy choice but they are more likely to as they have the finance to make that option possible. A single parent who relies on benefits may know which choice is healthy and may want to make that choice but will be forced to make a different choice due to finance. It is too simplistic to blame individuals for "making bad choices" without taking their financial position into consideration.
			(Total 3 marks evaluation)

Part B: Crime and the law in the United Kingdom

Question	General Marking Instructions for this type of question	Max marks	Specific Marking Instructions for this question
3. (c)	An analysis mark should be awarded where a candidate uses their knowledge and understanding/a source, to identify relevant components (e.g. of an idea, theory, argument, etc.) and clearly show at least one of the following: • links between different components • links between component(s) and the whole • links between components(s) and related concepts • similarities and contradictions • consistency and inconsistency • different views/interpretations • possible consequences/implications • the relative importance of components • understanding of underling order or structure Evaluation involves making a judgments based on criteria, drawing conclusions on the extent to which a view is supported by the evidence; counter-arguments including possible alternative interpretations; the overall impact/ significance of the factors when taken together; the relative importance of factors in relation to the context.	20	*Candidates can be credited in a number of ways up to a maximum of 20 marks.* **Credit reference to aspects of the following:** The Scottish government has introduced or extended a range of policies to reduce crime or improve crime prevention including: • policies to tackle antisocial behaviour • policies on counteracting the threat of terrorism • drugs — recovery and enforcement • new laws give greater protection to victims of forced marriage • tougher sanctions on crime linked to racial, religious or social prejudice • action on human trafficking • tough enforcement and prevention measures • protecting children from exploitation and dealing with extreme materials • policies on tackling prostitution and kerb-crawling offences • reducing re-offending • tackling serious organised crime in Scotland • reforming rape and sexual offences law • tackling misuse of firearms and air weapons in Scotland • youth justice measures — early intervention and tackling youth crime • introducing specialist drug courts • community payback orders • restriction of liberty orders • creation of Police Scotland Measures to implement some of the above were contained in the Criminal Justice and Licensing (Scotland) Act 2010.

Question		General Marking Instructions for this type of question	Max marks	Specific Marking Instructions for this question
3.	(c)	(continued) Credit responses that make reference to: • Theories of the causes of crime • Analysis of the importance of human nature as the main cause of crime • Balanced overall evaluative comment on the importance of human nature as the main cause of crime • Provide a clear, coherent line of argument Up to **8 marks** for KU (description, explanation and exemplification) and up to **12 marks** for analytical/evaluative comments. Award up to **6 marks** per point. Candidates should be credited up to **full marks** if they answer within a Scottish context only, a UK context only or refer to both Scotland and the UK as appropriate. Where a candidate makes more analytical/evaluative points than are required to gain the maximum allocation of **4 marks**, these can be credited as knowledge and understanding marks provided they meet the criteria for this.		In England and Wales, the Home Office claims emphasis is moving towards local community-based approaches to reducing crime, including improving crime prevention: • creating community triggers to deal with persistent antisocial behaviour • using community safety partnerships, and police and crime commissioners, • to work out local approaches to deal with issues, including antisocial behaviour, drug or alcohol misuse and re-offending • establishing the national referral mechanism (NRM) to make it easier for all the different agencies that could be involved in a trafficking case to co operate, share information about potential victims and access advice, accommodation and support • setting up the National Crime Agency (NCA) which will be a new body of operational crime fighters • creating street-level crime maps to give the public up-to-date, accurate information on what is happening on their streets so they can challenge the police on performance • creating the child sex offender disclosure scheme, which allows anyone concerned about a child to find out if someone in their life has a record for child sexual offences • legislating against hate crime • using football banning orders to stop potential trouble-makers from travelling to football matches both at home and abroad • legislation to prohibit cash payments to buy scrap metal and reforming the regulation of the scrap metal industry to stop unscrupulous dealers buying stolen metal The Antisocial Behaviour, Crime and Policing Bill was announced in May 2013. It aims to tackle a number of types of crime including antisocial behaviour, illegal use of firearms and organised crime. References can be made to Scottish and/or UK-based crime reduction policies. *Any other valid point that meets the criteria described in the general marking principles for this kind of question.* **Possible approaches to answering the question:** **Response 1** To try and reduce crime in Scotland the Scottish government has announced it will increase the mandatory sentence for carrying a knife from four to five years. The Scottish government hopes this will stop young people carrying knives *(1 mark KU)*. **Response 2** In Scotland there are many early intervention programmes that have been introduced to try and reduce crime. One early intervention programme is 'Kick It Kick Off' (KIKO) *(1 mark KU)*. This programme uses football to try and steer young people, many who have had problems at school or with the police, away from trouble *(1 mark KU)*. KIKO has reduced crime by providing a safe alternative to gang activity for many young Scots *(1 mark analysis)*. **(Total 3 marks — 2 marks KU, 1 mark analysis)**

Question		General Marking Instructions for this type of question	Max marks	Specific Marking Instructions for this question
3.	(c)	(continued)		**Response 3** The Criminal Justice and Licensing (Scotland) Act 2010 strengthened the law in terms of racial or religiously motivated crime. Now, where it has been proved that someone has committed an offence on grounds of race or religion (hate crimes), the courts must take this into account when handing out the sentence. This can lead to a longer custodial sentence or higher fine or a different type of punishment where appropriate *(3 marks KU)*. Although many people support tougher punishments for hate crimes, arguing this will make some people think twice before committing a crime, there are those who believe longer or tougher sentencing is the wrong approach. These people would argue that there is little evidence tougher sentencing for hate crimes works *(2 marks analysis)*. **(Total 5 marks – 3 marks KU, 2 marks analysis)**
3.	(d)	An analysis mark should be awarded where a candidate uses their knowledge and understanding/a source, to identify relevant components (e.g. of an idea, theory, argument, etc.) and clearly show at least one of the following: • links between different components • links between component(s) and the whole • links between components(s) and related concepts • similarities and contradictions • consistency and inconsistency • different views/interpretations • possible consequences/implications • the relative importance of components • understanding of underling order or structure Evaluation involves making a judgments based on criteria, drawing conclusions on the extent to which a view is supported by the evidence; counter-arguments including possible alternative interpretations; the overall impact/ significance of the factors when taken together; the relative importance of factors in relation to the context. Credit responses that make reference to: • Theories of the causes of crime • Analysis of the importance of human nature as the main cause of crime • Balanced overall evaluative comment on the importance of human nature as the main cause of crime • Provide a clear, coherent line of argument Up to **8 marks** for KU (description, explanation and exemplification) and up to **12 marks** for analytical/ evaluative comments.	20	*Candidates can be credited in a number of ways up to a maximum of 20 marks.* **Credit reference to aspects of the following:** • Human nature theory • Robert Merton/Strain theory of crime • Cultural deviance theory • Marxist theory • Charles Moore/Underclass theory • Conservative social breakdown theory • Reference to links between factors such as, drug/alcohol abuse, peer influence, family influence, etc. which don't mention theorists specifically should still be credited *Any other valid point that meets the criteria described in the general marking instructions for this kind of question.* **Possible approaches to answering this question:** **Response 1** There are many theories as to why people commit crimes; the individualist human nature theory is just one. For example, some people believe in Hobbes's belief that human nature explains crime; we are all essentially selfish and will break the law if given the chance. This could explain looting which took place during the 2011 London riots *(2 marks KU)*. **Response 2** There are many theories as to why people commit crimes; the individualist human nature theory is just one. For example, some people believe in Hobbes's belief that human nature explains crime; we are all essentially selfish and will break the law if given the chance. This could explain looting which took place during the 2011 London riots *(2 marks KU)*. This, however, cannot explain why many people chose not to take part in looting. Indeed, many people chose not to pursue their own self-interest instead they chose to help those whose shops were being looted so there are limits to the individualist human nature theory *(1 mark evaluative comment, 1 mark analysis)*. **(Total 4 marks – 2 marks KU, 1 mark analysis, 1 mark evaluation)**

Question	General Marking Instructions for this type of question	Max marks	Specific Marking Instructions for this question
3. (d)	(continued) Award up to **6 marks** per point. Candidates should be credited up to **full marks** if they answer within a Scottish context only, a UK context only or refer to both Scotland and the UK as appropriate. Where a candidate makes more analytical/evaluative points than are required to gain the maximum allocation of **4 marks**, these can be credited as knowledge and understanding marks provided they meet the criteria for this.		**Response 3** There are many theories of as to why people commit crimes; the individualist human nature theory is just one. For example, some people believe in Hobbes's belief that human nature explains crime; we are all essentially selfish and will break the law if given the chance. This could explain looting which took place during the 2011 London riots *(2 marks KU)*. Another explanation would be a Marxist explanation which believes that inequalities in society can explain crime. Those who are excluded from power and wealth will not respect the law and will commit crime. Evidence from the London riots showed that it was mostly people who were unemployed or "NEETs" who took part *(2 marks KU)*. Neither of these theories though can explain why some people choose not to commit crimes. Not everyone took part in the London riot looting and not all people from poor backgrounds are criminals. This suggests that other factors must play an important part in determining who will and who won't commit crime *(1 mark analysis, 1 mark evaluative comment)*. **(Total 6 marks — 4 marks KU, 1 mark analysis, 1 mark evaluation)** **Response 4** Some theories overlap in their explanations of the causes of crime. Charles Moore blames the growing "underclass" who he claims choose to live off benefits and have no stake in society, therefore do not care about obeying the law. This is an individualist view but a Marxist would also agree that capitalism from time to time creates a group of people who are marginalised. Human nature is not the sole cause; it is the economic system which creates criminals. **(Total 3 marks — 1 mark KU, 1 mark analysis, 1 mark evaluation)** **Response 5** Overall, there are many different theories of crime, each with their strengths and weaknesses. Some theories, such as social breakdown, are good at explaining crimes relating to gangs and drug use. But this theory has little to say about crimes committed by the better off in society. Marxist theories are better at explaining corporate crime but are weaker at explaining why some individuals choose not to commit crime. In conclusion, it would seem to be fair to say that human nature plays some part in explaining crime but does not explain why certain groups in society are more likely than others to be involved in crime. A complex mixture of social and economic factors is responsible for the criminal behaviour, or lack of it, shown by each individual *(4 marks evaluation)*.

Section 3 — International Issues

Question	General Marking Instructions for this type of question	Max marks	Specific Marking Instructions for this question
4.	The candidate is required to interpret/evaluate up to three complex sources of information detecting and explaining the extent of objectivity. In order to achieve credit candidates must show evidence which supports the extent of accuracy in a given viewpoint. Award up to 3 marks for: • appropriate use of evidence depending on the quality of the explanation and the synthesis of the evidence for any one explanation of the extent of objectivity. • For **full marks** candidates must refer to all sources in their answer. • For **full marks** candidates must make an overall judgment as to the extent of the accuracy of the given statement. • accuracy of the statement. Award up to **3 marks** for: • appropriate use of evidence depending on the quality of the explanation and the synthesis of the evidence for any one explanation of the extent of objectivity. • For **full marks** candidates must refer to all sources in their answer. • For **full marks** candidates must make an overall judgment as to the extent of the accuracy of the given statement. • accuracy of the statement. • Candidates may be awarded up to a maximum of **2 marks** for incorporating an evaluation of the reliability of the sources in their explanations although this is not mandatory. Maximum of **6 marks** if no overall judgement made on extent of accuracy.	8	*Candidates can be credited in a number of ways **up to a maximum of 8 marks**.* **Evidence that supports the view (*"Russia effectively protects the rights of its citizens"*)** Examples of the types of evidence that support the view include: • Source C, there has been an extension of jury trials across the country • Source C, the death penalty has been suspended • Source A, no executions since 1996 • Source C, fewer complaints, drop from 58,000 to 24,000 in two years • Source C, right of protest is protected by law • Source A, campaign groups had the freedom to challenge the law in the courts • Source B, better rights than China or Saudi Arabia **Response 1** The rights of Russians are well protected as in Source A campaign groups could take the government to court, which is an important right. This is supported by Source C which states that the right to protest is protected and that registering as a foreign agent did not affect this right *(2 marks, evidence linked from two sources)*. **Evidence that opposes the view (*"Russia effectively protects the rights of its citizens"*)** • Source A, groups forced to register as "foreign agents" which is seen as traitor by Russian people • Source A, media campaign to discredit groups • Source A, wide definition means a large number of campaign groups can be included • Source A, leaders prosecuted and groups with no option but to disband • Source A, court decision supports government, many complain about courts (56% Source C) • Source B, Russia compares badly to other major countries in Political Rights index meaning poor freedom of speech, participation, etc.(backed by information from Source A) • Source B, Russia rating on the PRI has decreased since 1997, meaning rights are not well protected **Response 2** The rights of Russians are not effectively protected by the government as Russia's rating (Source B) is the second lowest it could be. It has also been in decline from 3 to 6 in recent years. This shows that the right to participate and freedom of speech are not adequately protected. This is supported by Source A which shows that anyone campaigning for improvements has effectively been discredited as a foreign spy by the government. The right to protest may be protected by law (Source C) but this won't be effective if the public are against "Foreign Agents" *(3 marks, relevant evidence from all three sources with evaluative comment)*. *Candidates may also be credited **up to 2 marks** on any comment/analysis of the origin and reliability of the source.*

Question		General Marking Instructions for this type of question	Max marks	Specific Marking Instructions for this question
4.		(continued)		Although Source C is fairly up to date (2014) it is unreliable as it comes from Sputniknews.com which is owned and operated by the Russian government and so will present information in a biased way to make them look better **(2 marks)**.

- Source A is unreliable as it is adapted **(1 mark)**.
- Source A is unreliable as it is adapted. We have no idea how much of this article has been adapted. We also have no idea who adapted it therefore we cannot be sure that it accurately reflects the views of the Human Rights watch group **(2 marks)**.
- Statistics in Source B are up to date (2015) **(0 marks)**.
- Statistics in Source B are up to date (2015) and so give a fairly up to date picture of the position of Russia compared to other countries **(1 mark)**.
- Source C is unreliable as it is adapted. We have no idea how much of this article has been adapted. We also have no idea who adapted it therefore we cannot be sure that it accurately reflects the views of the original author **(2 marks)**.

For full marks, candidates must make an overall judgment as to the extent of the accuracy of the given statement.

Accept overall judgements similar to:
- On the whole, the evidence suggests that Russia does not protect the rights of its citizens **(0 marks)**.
- The statement is largely untrue as the government have made it very difficult for any campaign groups to operate. This means that opposition to their policies is being silenced. Although jury trials are more widespread and there have been no executions since 1996, basic political rights are being denied. The Political Rights Index supports this conclusion as Russia's rating is declining over time and is only better than China and Saudi Arabia **(2 marks)**.
- Russia is doing well with Human Rights as the EU praised them for not executing anyone recently **(1 mark)**.
- The statement is true to a certain extent, as there have been fewer complaints recently but they rank poorly on the political rights index **(1 mark)**.
- The statement is true to a certain extent **(0 marks)**.

Part A: World Powers

Question		General Marking Instructions for this type of question	Max marks	Specific Marking Instructions for this question
5.	(a)	Evaluation involves making judgments, drawing conclusions on the extent to which a view is supported by the evidence; the relative importance of factors; counter-arguments including possible alternative interpretations; the overall impact/significance of the factors when taken together; the relative importance of factors in relation to the context.	12	*Candidates can be credited in a number of ways up to a maximum of 12 marks.* **World Power Choice: Brazil** **Possible approaches to answering the question:** **Response 1** Within Brazil there is a widening gap between rich and poor with currently 16 million Brfazilians experiencing poverty and living on less than $44 a month *(1 mark KU)*. One key policy to tackle growing poverty is through the welfare strategy of the Bolsa Familia which provides financial support to those families with children living below the poverty line *(1 mark KU)*. The programme has grown rapidly and in the past ten years, the number of families receiving payments has risen from 3.6 million to 13.8 million covering nearly a quarter of Brazil's population *(1 mark KU)*.

Question		General Marking Instructions for this type of question	Max marks	Specific Marking Instructions for this question
5.	(a)	(continued) Credit responses that make reference to: • Role of world power in international relations • Evaluation of the importance of world power in international relations Up to **8 marks** for KU (description, explanation and exemplification) and up to **4 marks** for evaluative comments. Award up to **6 marks** per point. Where a candidate makes more evaluative points than are required to gain the maximum allocation of **4 marks**, these can be credited as knowledge and understanding marks provided they meet the criteria for this.		However, the payment is conditional and is only guaranteed if the children are kept in school and get vaccinated. Some also argue the payment is too little to live on with payments of 70 reis a person to any family below the poverty line of 140 reis a month, hence not really helping end poverty *(2 marks evaluation)*. Furthermore, some Brazilians have reported that they have tried to claim the benefits paid out by Bolsa Familia and have failed to receive any money from the Government. Critics claim that this policy has had limited success and non-payment is often down to the corruption of local officials *(1 mark KU, 1 mark evaluation)*. **(Total 7 marks — 4 marks KU, 3 marks evaluation)** **Response 2** The number of American citizens without private healthcare insurance or employer-based coverage has increased with currently 47 million people uninsured. The numbers of uninsured Americans increased as access to healthcare became increasingly unaffordable and many employers were reducing the coverage they provided to workers. To assist the 15% of the population who are currently not covered by their employers or by US healthcare programs such as Medicaid, Barack Obama introduced the healthcare reform law which aims to extend health coverage to those who do not have it at a more affordable rate *(3 marks KU)*. Since The Affordable Health Care Act was introduced on October 1st 2013, over 1 million people are estimated to have signed up however, this is a lower up take than expected, showing the policy has had limited success *(1 mark KU, 1 mark evaluation)*. **(Total 5 marks — 4 marks KU, 1 mark evaluation)** **Response 3** The plan to make all Americans take out health care has proved controversial and sign up rates have differed across the states with many Republicans claiming it could end up being very expensive for individuals and firms. Healthcare reform has generated heated debate in the USA as many Republicans worry it will lead to tax increases that are unnecessary, leading to inevitable failure of the policy *(1 mark KU, 2 marks evaluation)*. However, the act is showing encouraging signs of success as people who have pre-existing conditions who previously would have experienced difficulty obtaining coverage, are now covered under the new proposals of 'Obamacare' *(1 mark KU, 1 mark evaluation)*. **(Total 5 marks — 2 marks KU, 3 marks evaluation)**
5.	(b)	Evaluation involves making judgments, drawing conclusions on the extent to which a view is supported by the evidence; the relative importance of factors; counter-arguments including possible alternative interpretations; the overall impact/significance of the factors when taken together; the relative importance of factors in relation to the context. Credit responses that make reference to: • Role of world power in international relations • Evaluation of the importance of world power in international relations	12	*Candidates can be credited in a number of ways up to a maximum of 12 marks.* Depending on the world power chosen, candidates may make reference to any relevant aspects, such as: • nature of political system • extent of democracy • constitutional arrangements • opportunities to form, join, campaign for political parties • role of electoral system • extent of human and political rights • role of media • opportunities to take part in pressure group/interest group activities

Question		General Marking Instructions for this type of question	Max marks	Specific Marking Instructions for this question
5.	(b)	(continued) Up to **8 marks** for KU (description, explanation and exemplification) and up to **4 marks** for evaluative comments. Award up to **6 marks** per point. Where a candidate makes more evaluative points than are required to gain the maximum allocation of **4 marks**, these can be credited as knowledge and understanding marks provided they meet the criteria for this.		**In the USA:** **Response 1** Citizens have a wide range of opportunities to put forward their views. One way of having your views represented is through voting for elected officials. The US Constitution guarantees the right to vote for a large range of political offices including the President of the USA, both houses of Congress and a wide range of state and local officials. Competing parties present candidates for all these positions, voters have a free choice. Although there are many opportunities for US citizens to express their views through voting, turnout in elections, especially at state and county levels, is often low. This may be because many people (especially ethnic minority groups) believe their views will not be represented. (Total 4 marks – 2 marks KU, 2 marks evaluation) **In China:** **Response 2** In theory, China is a multi-party socialist state. In the highest bodies of the Chinese government, nine political parties are represented, including the Communist party. However, the views of Chinese citizens are not well-represented as the Communist party is by far the largest party and the other eight parties are only allowed to operate by permission of the CPC and will not disagree or act as an opposition to the views of the CPC. It is also the case that Chinese citizens are not allowed to vote directly for the higher bodies in the political system as the higher bodies are chosen by the body below. Chinese citizens only have the right to directly elect representatives at the very lowest "village" level, which has only limited influence over local issues. (Total 6 marks – 3 marks KU, 3 marks evaluation) **In South Africa:** **Response 3** Since the end of apartheid, all citizens have had the right to vote and there are a wide range of political parties which South Africans can choose from. Over the last 20 years, many new political parties have been formed, showing that there are opportunities for different views to be represented. In 2014, the fifth election was held since the end of apartheid and which allows all South Africans to vote. Elections are held every five years for the National Assembly and the provincial legislatures. The African National Congress is the main party in South Africa and it won over 60% of the vote. All the other parties received fewer votes, with the Democratic Alliance receiving just over 20% of the vote and the newly formed Economic Freedom Fighters receiving just over 6% of the vote. (Total 4 marks – 3 marks KU, 1 mark evaluation) *Any other valid point that meets the criteria described in the general marking principles for this kind of question.*

Part B: World Issues

Question		General Marking Instructions for this type of question	Max marks	Specific Marking Instructions for this question
5.	(c)	Evaluation involves making judgments based on criteria, drawing conclusions on the extent to which a view is supported by the evidence; counter-arguments including possible alternative interpretations; the overall impact/significance of the factors when taken together; the relative importance of factors in relation to the context. Credit responses that make reference to: • A significant international issue • An evaluation of the impact of the issue on different groups in different countries Up to **8 marks** for KU (description, explanation and exemplification) and up to **4 marks** for evaluative comments. Award up to **6 marks** per point. Candidates may make reference to any world issues the impact which extends beyond the boundaries of any single country. This impact may be regional or global in scale. Where a candidate makes more evaluative points than are required to gain the maximum allocation of **4 marks**, these can be credited as knowledge and understanding marks provided they meet the criteria for this.	12	*Candidates can be credited in a number of ways **up to a maximum of 12 marks**.* **Credit reference to aspects of the following:** • war — Afghanistan, Libya, Syria • nuclear weapons — North Korea • borders — Middle East • economic difficulties — EU countries (Portugal, Ireland, Italy, Greece, Spain) • factors which limit development *Any other valid point that meets the criteria described in the general marking instructions for this kind of question.* **Possible approaches to answering this question:** **Response 1** The Israeli-Palestine conflict has been going on for a long time. The conflict involves both sides recognising each other as a country and agreeing on which territories, e.g. Jerusalem should belong to Israel or a Palestine state *(1 mark KU)*. **Response 2** The Israeli-Palestine conflict has been going on for a long time. The conflict involves both sides recognising each other as a country and agreeing on which territories, e.g. Jerusalem should belong to Israel or a Palestine state. The conflict has resulted in around 16,000 people being killed, the majority of these are Palestinians *(2 marks KU)*. The Israeli economy fails to attract foreign investment due to this conflict which seriously hinders economic growth and leads to a much lower standard of living for its people. However, this problem is far more severe for the Palestinians who live in the Gaza Strip who are often forced to rely on foreign aid for survival *(1 mark KU, 2 marks evaluation)*. (Total 5 marks — 3 marks KU, 2 marks evaluation) **Response 3** The areas known as "the West Bank" and the Gaza strip are the two most disputed areas in the conflict. The Palestinians refer to this as Occupied Palestinian Territory whereas the Israelis say these are "disputed territories" as no one owned them when Israel captured them in 1967 *(2 marks KU)*. The Gaza Strip which is only 25km long has very high levels of poverty and unemployment *(1 mark evaluation)*. Israel blockaded the Gaza Strip in 2007 in order to curb the influence of the political group Hamas. Israel maintains the blockade has at no point caused a humanitarian crisis but aid agencies have criticised the conditions people have had to live in, in particular water supplies and toilet conditions *(1 mark KU, 1 mark evaluation)*. It is clear that innocent people are suffering in these two areas. As well as many violent deaths, health and education services are badly hampered leading to a great deal of avoidable suffering and an inability to create prosperity through investment and growth *(1 mark KU, 1 mark evaluation)*. (Total 7 marks — 4 marks KU, 3 marks evaluation)

Question		General Marking Instructions for this type of question	Max marks	Specific Marking Instructions for this question
5.	(d)	Evaluation involves making judgments based on criteria, drawing conclusions on the extent to which a view is supported by the evidence; counter-arguments including possible alternative interpretations; the overall impact/significance of the factors when taken together; the relative importance of factors in relation to the context. Credit responses that make reference to: • Ways in which international organisations can address a significant world issue • An evaluation of the effectiveness of international organisations in addressing a significant world issue Up to **8 marks** for KU (description, explanation and exemplification) and up to **4 marks** for evaluative comments. Award up to **6 marks** per point. Candidates may make reference to any world issues the impact which extends beyond the boundaries of any single country. This impact may be regional or global in scale. Where a candidate makes more evaluative points than are required to gain the maximum allocation of **4 marks**, these can be credited as knowledge and understanding marks provided they meet the criteria for this.	12	*Candidates can be credited in a number of ways **up to a maximum of 12 marks**.* • World Issue: international terrorism (UN/NATO) • World Issue: developing world poverty (UN agencies/NGOs) • World Issue: nuclear proliferation (UN) • World Issue: global economic crisis (EU/World Bank/IMF) *Any other valid point that meets the criteria described in the general marking instructions for this kind of question.* **Possible approaches to answering this question: (Terrorism/NATO)** **Response 1** NATO has been involved in the Afghanistan war since 2001. This was an attempt to rid the country of the al Qaeda and the Taliban after the attacks on 9/11 *(1 mark KU)*. **Response 2** NATO has been involved in the Afghanistan war since 2001. This was an attempt to rid the country of al Qaeda and the Taliban after the attacks on 9/11 *(1 mark KU)*. This was the first time NATO had been involved in a conflict in Asia and Operation ISAF attempted to make Afghanistan a democracy with its own elected government *(1 mark KU)*. The operation was effective in the early days, successfully driving out al Qaeda but the Taliban has been much more resilient *(1 mark evaluative comment)*. (Total 3 marks — 2 marks KU, 1 mark evaluation) **Response 3** NATO has been involved in the Afghanistan war since 2001. This was an attempt to rid the country of al Qaeda and the Taliban after the attacks on 9/11. Over 150,000 NATO troops have served in Afghanistan, the bulk of these have been American soldiers. In 2010 the US had a 'surge' where it sent an extra 33,000 troops *(2 marks KU)*. ISAF has been successful in tackling al Qaeda. Afghanistan is no longer a 'safe haven' and Osama Bin Laden has been killed *(1 mark evaluation)*. However, the Afghanistan government has been weak and the Taliban have not been defeated. Most NATO troops pulled out in 2014 and many believe that it is only a matter of time until the Taliban re-emerge. NATOs success may well only be short term *(2 marks evaluation)*. (Total 5 marks — 2 marks KU, 3 marks evaluation) **Response 4** Over 3,000 NATO soldiers have been killed and there have been many civilian casualties too. While education and health systems have been created, the cost of the war in terms of casualties and finance has led some people to question how effective the intervention has been. (Total 2 marks — 1 mark KU, 1 mark evaluation)

Acknowledgements

Permission has been sought from all relevant copyright holders and Hodder Gibson is grateful for the use of the following:

Source B: Charts adapted from 'National Voting Intention: the impact of the first debate — How would you vote if there were a General Election tomorrow' taken from 'General Election 2010, The Leaders' Debates, The worms' final verdict — lessons to be learned' 30 April 2010, by Ipsos Mori. Chart A: 'Before the first debate: 21—23 March' (Base: All certain to vote = 833 unweighted; data collected among 1,503 British adults 18+, 19th—22nd March 2010). Chart B: 'After the first debate: 18—19 April' (Base: All certain to vote = 802 unweighted; data collected among 1,253 British adults 18+, 18th—19th April 2010). Reproduced by kind permission of Ipsos MORI (SQP page 3);

Source A: An extract from http://www.bbc.co.uk/news/uk-scotland-scotland-politics-21954909 © BBC (2015 page 4);

Source B: The graph 'Percentage (%) who smoke in Scotland by economic status (2012)' taken from page 10 of 'Scotland's People Annual Report: Results from 2012 Scottish Household Survey' (http://www.scotland.gov.uk/ Publications/2013/08/6973/10) © Crown Copyright. Contains public sector information licensed under the Open Government Licence v3.0. (http://www.nationalarchives.gov.uk/doc/open-government-licence/version/3/) (2015 page 5);

Source C: The graph 'Percentage (%) of 13 and 15 year olds who smoke regularly 1990—2013 and 2014—2018 (projected)' taken from 'ASH Scotland: Young people & tobacco' March 2015 (http://www.ashscotland.org.uk/ media/3322/young_people_and_tobacco_March2010.pdf) © ASH Scotland (2015 page 5).